Intel® Trusted Execution Technology for Server Platforms

A Guide to More Secure Datacenters

William Futral

James Greene

apress
open

Intel® Trusted Execution Technology for Server Platforms

William Futral and James Greene

President and Publisher: Paul Manning
Lead Editors: Jeffrey Pepper (Apress); Patrick Hauke (Intel)
Coordinating Editor: Mark Powers
Cover Designer: Anna Ishchenko

Distributed to the book trade worldwide by Springer Science+Business Media New York, 233 Spring Street, 6th Floor, New York, NY 10013. Phone 1-800-SPRINGER, fax (201) 348-4505, e-mail orders-ny@springer-sbm.com, or visit www.springeronline.com.

For information on translations, please e-mail rights@apress.com, or visit www.apress.com.

About ApressOpen

What Is ApressOpen?

- ApressOpen is an open access book program that publishes high-quality technical and business information.

- ApressOpen eBooks are available for global, free, noncommercial use.

- ApressOpen eBooks are available in PDF, ePub, and Mobi formats.

- The user friendly ApressOpen free eBook license is presented on the copyright page of this book.

To my wife, Mary Jo. Without your support, encouragement, inspiration, patience, love, and sacrifice, this book would not have been possible. So thank you from the bottom of my heart.

—William Futral

To Mari, Sarah, and Emma. I couldn't succeed without you and your patience. Many thanks and much love to my family for supporting me as I pursue my professional interests, no matter how odd these interests may seem to them and the hours I apply to them.

—James Greene

Contents at a Glance

Contents

Foreword

I can practically see the scenario: somewhere in the upper echelons of what is the Intel think tank there is a heated meeting underway, it's about Intel's Trusted Execution Technology (Intel TXT). Everyone involved in the technology—from design and integration teams to sales and marketing executives—is present. There is a United Nations feel about the place, with differing opinions and points of view on just about every aspect of Intel TXT. Then, there is a question about implementation… Silence. All heads turn toward Bill Futral.

There is no question that Bill is an authority when it comes to hardware security. That being said, the journey that has led our team to work so closely with the likes of Jim Greene, Bill Futral, and other gurus at Intel on this question of trusted hardware has been challenging, controversial, and at times a bit scary. About ten years ago, I was involved with a small group of individuals that had developed a set of tools based on an ambitious premise. If only there was a way to collect, store, and query every event from every system, everywhere. This should enable us to detect, correlate, and in some cases anticipate security incidents more accurately than ever before. What I didn't realize back then was that Security Information and Event Management (SIEM) would soon become a critical component of information security programs everywhere, and well on its way to becoming a billion-dollar industry.

A large service provider noticed what we were up to and came knocking on our door. They figured that if they could deliver world-class network services from their Network Operations Center (NOC) using traditional IP monitoring tools, they should be able to use our security-event monitoring software to build a Security Operations Center (SOC) to help meet their customer's growing security needs. It made sense to me, so I took the red pill and plugged into the service provider matrix. What they didn't tell me was that they had an ambitious idea of their own that would flip traditional datacenter security on its head; they called it Cloud Computing.

This new product offering consisted of shared physical infrastructure that the Provider would make directly available to Subscribers through a web portal. The idea was to allow these Subscribers to access, provision, and manage their own virtual infrastructure with a pay-as-you-go model, running on the Provider's shared hardware. This presented a unique twist to security implementation that was foreign to me. As a security practitioner, considerations such as multitenancy, shared infrastructure, virtual domains, and service delivery had typically been someone else's problem. At first, I couldn't quite wrap my head around how anyone in their right mind would give up complete control of their infrastructure to someone that was telling them they will be sharing hardware with other users *and* that they couldn't know who these other users were. From a security perspective, this was crazy talk!

We deployed every conventional security control (and some not so conventional), implemented every policy and procedure we could think of, and managed all of it from our SOC leveraging one of the largest SIEM implementations in the world. We had accomplished a lot of good things, weaving security into every aspect of the Cloud. Then one day, my Director at the time, current CEO Robert Rounsavall, was giving a tour of our facility to federal customers, explaining all of our security services. They had recently heard reports of some supply-chain incidents and BIOS-level attacks, so they asked us what we were doing about protecting our hardware platform. I had also heard accounts of foreign hardware mysteriously appearing on the system board of security appliances shipped abroad. The devices had supposedly been "held up in customs for a few weeks." At the time, we hadn't been doing much of anything to address this threat, so we put in place manual processes to update the firmware of every platform we provisioned, and revisited our acquisition practices to make sure we were buying the best possible equipment with the lowest risk of compromise. The world was starting to uncover one of the darkest little secrets being kept by Cloud Providers: There was absolutely no way to measure, validate, or automate anything at the hardware level.

Strategically, it was difficult to raise awareness about the risk because we knew so little about how to effectively address it. While upper management was struggling with defining and quantifying the threat, we began to see growing industry concerns. Organizations such as the National Institute of Standards and Technology (NIST), the Trusted Computing Group (TCG), and the Open Data Center Alliance (ODCA) began to publish best practices and usage models around provisioning hardware, trusted computing, and data boundaries. Meanwhile, I found myself running the SOC at a large Cloud Provider, thinking about the ramifications of having almost zero visibility into the integrity of the underlying infrastructure. Even more disconcerting was that we were performing live incident response on virtual machines (VMs), not knowing exactly where these VMs lived, where they had been in the recent past, or even which other customers were sharing physical servers with these compromised systems! And if I didn't know—surely the customer had no idea. Tactically, this became a nightmare that kept me up at night. A nightmare that usually played out like one of those worst-case scenario studies by the NSA asking questions such as: What if a nuclear weapon was covertly smuggled into the country? What if the water supply was secretly infected with a deadly bacteria? What if all our Cloud servers were rooted at the BIOS level?

Enter Intel TXT. My first exposure to Intel TXT was in 2010, after participating in a meeting with a couple of Intel visionaries and some VMware experts. Finally, I thought, something practical that actually measures firmware and embedded code on servers. After spending three years skirting the question of infrastructure security and hardware integrity, ignoring what I thought was a huge blind spot in security monitoring, it was time to implement this new hardware-based security technology. What this meant for us was finding a way to not only surface this newfound hardware trust data but integrate it into our traditional security tools such as SIEM for visibility, policy enforcement for blocking, and intrusion analysis for correlation.

In addition to measuring the integrity of the underlying hardware, we also realized that this technology could be used to address some other major areas of concern. For example, if we could devise an automated way to capture and monitor these measurements, we could use them to uniquely identify each physical server, allowing us to easily connect the dots up through the hypervisor and back to the VM. Imagine being able to identify, in real time, the location of every VM in the Cloud and track its movements over time. Now *that* was something to write home about!

This demanded further real-world exploration, so I hung up my incident-handling jump bag and decided to work directly with customers that were attempting to securely and responsibly move assets into the Cloud. As I further explored the hardware-attack surface associated with initiatives such as Bring Your Own Device (BYOD) and all the different flavors of Cloud cropping up, it seemed like there was no end to the vectors from which exploits can influence the way hardware behaves, and therefore everything that rides on top. Recently, with the help of Intel and a handful of pioneering Cloud Providers, we have had some exciting success stories, but there is still quite a bit of unchartered territory.

The importance of this book and the further development of Intel TXT cannot be overstated. We are currently witnessing a shift in paradigm where the Cloud's core function of abstracting software from hardware is no longer cool enough to make us forget that hardware still exists. The fact that everything everywhere is actually running on some hardware platform somewhere, can no longer be ignored. Intel TXT is one of those technologies that will help us find solid ground in an industry that has already spent too much time in the Cloud!

—Albert Caballero
CTO, Trapezoid

About the Authors

William (Bill) Futral is a senior staff architect in the Digital Enterprise Group at Intel Corporation. In his 20 years with the company, he has played significant roles in the introduction of emerging technologies such as Intel Trusted Execution Technology (Intel TXT), virtualization, Intelligent I/O (I²O), InfiniBand, and other major initiatives. Bill is the author of the book *InfiniBand Architecture: Development and Deployment—A Strategic Guide to Server I/O Solutions* (Intel Press, 2001) and has authored many other technical publications and design guides. Bill has served on various international standards committees, including ARINC, IEEE, and the American National Standards Institute (ANSI).

James Greene is a product marketing engineer for Security Technologies at Intel. In this role, he is responsible for the definition of products and usage models for datacenter and cloud security solutions such as Intel Trusted Execution Technology. He came to Intel when the company purchased Conformative Systems in 2005. At Conformative, James led all product marketing activities for the XML processing appliance portfolio. Prior to that, James held several leadership roles in marketing, strategy, market development, and business and technology planning for Compaq's and Hewlett-Packard's enterprise server, workstation, and storage business units.

Acknowledgments

The authors gratefully acknowledge the contributions, edits, and suggestions from our external and internal reviewers, particularly our Intel colleagues Patrick Hauke, Lynn Comp, Michael Hall, Iddo Kadim, Steve Bekefi, Tracie Zenti, Sham Data, Raghu Yeluri, Alex Eydelberg, Will Arthur, Mahesh Natu, and Jeff Pishny, and external reviewers Albert Caballero, Michael Dyer, Hemma Prafullchandra, Merritte Stidston, John McAuley, Alex Rodriguez, Pete Nicoletti, Murugiah Souppaya, Gargi Mitra Keeling, and Robert Rounsavall. Their time, guidance, and expertise were invaluable in the development of this material. We would also like to recognize the many direct and indirect contributions of the Intel TXT development, solutions, sales, and marketing teams and the ecosystem partners and initial customers that allowed us to cultivate the insights and experiences that inform so much of the material in this book.

Introduction

While there are numerous papers and other forms of documentation on Intel® Trusted Execution Technology (Intel® TXT), most of them focus on helping the platform designer and operating system vendor (OSV) implement the technology on a hardware or software platform. There are, however, a small amount of engineering, marketing and positioning materials that focus on the outcome or the use of the technology that would be helpful to an IT professional. Often though, these materials are more objective than subjective. That is, they tell the designer or implementer what they can do, but not necessarily what they should do, or why they would want to select one option over another. In the practice of making real use of new technologies, this gap creates a problem.

Our experience has shown that when a platform arrives at the datacenter, there is typically very little information to guide the system administrator to make the best use of new capabilities such as Intel TXT. While Intel is well versed in collaborative dialog with our core audience of platform architects, OS architects, and software developers regarding implementation details, the Intel TXT enablement experience exposed us more forcefully to a new audience—and a new opportunity. We continually get questions from IT managers and cloud solutions architects wanting to know how this technology is and should be employed, in order that they can evaluate which options they should implement in their own environments. Hardware and software designers are also inquisitive about how the datacenters deploy the technology, what issues they face, and which features are important to them.

Thus it was obvious that there needs to be a book to provide a more complete picture, starting with why the technology is important, what the hardware does, and then work its way up the stack specifying the roles of the OEM, datacenter, OSV, and ISV. In short, our goal became: create a book that takes the mystery out of this new technology—from architecture to deployment. This publication also allows us the opportunity to raise visibility for emerging threats, while being in the envious position of being able to raise awareness of solutions based on products that our core audience is quite likely already buying (such as Intel TXT enabled servers and operating systems or hypervisors). Happily, we can also help note that solutions based on this technology are also integrated or enabled at "trivial" extra costs such as the $30-50 cost of adding a TPM module to some OEM servers. In short, these solutions are really near at hand, it is just a matter of getting the word out and helping show the methods and benefits!

This book provides a comprehensive guide for the datacenter as well as providing additional contextual insight for the platform and software suppliers. Thus the first half of this book explains what the technology does and why it works, explains how attestation works, discusses the value of various features, and walks the reader through the process of enabling the technology, creating launch policies, and selecting the best policy for the datacenter. And it does so in the context of explaining what choices are possible and the key considerations behind them. In short, the first half is largely about implementation—the "what" and "how" of Intel TXT.

The second half of this book is designed to provide an overview of the big-picture "why" of implementing Intel TXT. It focuses on the use models—what operational, security and business benefits can be derived from using it? It focuses on the ecosystem requirements—the key hardware, software and services that are needed today and in the future—to make use of Intel TXT in the cloud or enterprise. These discussions are intended to help the IT administrator or enterprise security architect assess the capabilities of the technologies and dependencies of the use models against their business needs. And it closes with a discussion of the future.

No IT manager or architect wants to dedicate their time and resources to build or deploy a one-off solution. It is essential to not only explain the capabilities (and limitations) of today, but to provide insight into where this foundation may lead and how that may also map into rapidly evolving business needs. The intention here is to help IT and security leaders identify and establish new opportunities to solve security challenges of today, and also position themselves to use enhanced security capabilities to more fully enable and drive the enterprise of the future.

Intel TXT is being deployed today by companies across the globe and in many industries. Are they undertaking wholesale "ripping and replacing" of IT infrastructure to gain the protections and capabilities enabled by Intel TXT? Absolutely not. That is not how IT works. No, instead they are deploying their new server installations with Intel TXT activated and built and targeted to key visibility, control and compliance use models—typically for their cloud infrastructures. In effect, they are establishing new, more secure pools within their existing infrastructure that are more suitable for hosting their more sensitive or regulated workloads. This type of optimized deployment model is also a well-worn IT practice for targeting resources and utilizing the optimal platform to host them.

These earlier adopters are gaining hard-earned benefits today and setting the stage for a more secure future for their businesses. They are learning much from this process as they pioneer solutions even as the market and technologies mature (and in fact they help shape the direction of the maturation by working with Intel and others to implement these solutions). Our objective with this book is to help share the groundwork of experts and pioneers and to lower the barriers to implementation so that these trust-based solutions can deliver value much more broadly through the industry.

■ ■ ■

CHAPTER 1

Introduction to Trust and Intel® Trusted Execution Technology

Every contrivance of man, every tool, every instrument, every utensil, every article designed for use, of each and every kind, evolved from very simple beginnings.

—Robert Collier

Intel® Trusted Execution Technology (Intel® TXT) is a technology that uses enhanced processor architecture, special hardware, and associated firmware that enable certain Intel processors to provide the basis for many new innovations in secure computing. It is especially well suited for cloud computing and other uses where data integrity is paramount. Its primary goal is to establish an environment that is known to be trusted from the very start and further provide system software with the means to provide a more secure system and better protect data integrity. This is essential in that if the platform cannot be protected, then the data it will store or process cannot really be protected. At a minimum, this technology provides discrete integrity measurements that can prove or disprove a software component's integrity. These software components include, but are not limited to, code (such as BIOS, firmware, and operating system), platform and software configuration, events, state, status, and policies.

By providing a hardware-based security foundation rooted in the processor and chipset, Intel TXT provides greater protection for information that is used and stored on servers. A key aspect of that protection is the provision of an isolated execution environment and associated sections of memory where operations can be conducted on sensitive data, isolated from the rest of the system. Likewise, Intel TXT provides for sealed storage where sensitive data such as encryption keys can be securely kept to shield them from being compromised during an attack by malicious code. Attestation mechanisms verify that the system has correctly invoked Intel TXT to make sure that code is, in fact, executing in this protected environment.

This book describes how this technology can benefit the datacenter, and it specifically addresses the concerns of the cloud service provider and the cloud service client. The goals of this book are as follows:

- To explain what this technology does and its underlying principles

- To describe the roles and responsibilities for enabling and using this technology

- To guide the system administrator in establishing the right launch control policy

- To discuss how software (local and remote) can take advantage of this technology

- To look at some current and future innovations and how they apply to public and private clouds

Clearly these are important topics, so let's get started!

Why More Security?

Intel Trusted Execution Technology is relatively new for servers. It was initially developed for desktop and mobile computing platforms. It first debuted in servers in 2010 as attacks on datacenters started to escalate and calls for platform hardening formalized. For quite some time, server platforms were thought to be immune from attacks because they are typically kept in secure rooms and managed by highly skilled professionals. That is no longer sufficient. The frequency of attacks against datacenters is growing at astounding rates and those attacks are increasingly likely to have come from organized crime, corporate competitors, or sponsored by foreign governments with very sophisticated methodologies and deep resources.[1] Corporate executives worry that a breach could be very costly—both socially and economically, in the face of new regulations and stiffer penalties for failing to protect personal information.

Andy Grove, one of the Intel's founders, wrote the book *Only the Paranoid Survive* (Doubleday Business, 1996). This book is about recognizing inflection points and taking action. Server security is definitely at one of those inflection points. A successful attack could do significant damage to a company, regardless of whether that company is providing the service or using it—especially if adversaries can demonstrate that the company failed to use available security precautions. But it doesn't even take a successful attack. Just the failure to use available security precautions, or to make them available to your customers, could do irreparable harm.

Furthermore, this need for vigilance and caution doesn't only apply to business environments. The individual making online purchases, retail companies using cloud computing services, and cloud service providers all want more assurances that transactions and data are protected.

The answer is a higher level of security, better ability to mitigate attacks, and the means to prove those capabilities are enforced. Intel Trusted Execution Technology (or Intel TXT) can now be a significant part of that solution.

Types of Attacks

Bad people do bad things for all sorts of reasons. Some try to prevent use of the platform (denial of service, a.k.a. DoS attacks), some want to destroy or corrupt data, and others want to steal data. They will attack data in flight, at rest, and in use.

Data-in-flight refers to the transmission of data from one place to another. Using a secure channel that encrypts data during transport helps defend against in-flight attacks, but one also has to make sure that the recipient is the intended recipient and guard against replay attacks and the man-in-the-middle attacks. A replay attack is where an attacker intercepts a transmission and resends a copy of that transmission at a later time to fool the recipient into thinking it came from an authorized source portraying a real transaction. The man-in-the-middle attack is where an entity inserts itself into the communication link, forwarding transactions between the two endpoints, and thus gaining access to the privileged information. For this case, entity A starts a session with the attacker (the "man in the middle") thinking it is a session with entity B. The attacker then starts a secure session with the intended entity B, claiming it is entity A. The attacker is now able to steal or modify the data being transmitted between A and B.

Data-at-rest refers to the storage of data. Encrypting the data before storing on disk is a growing practice, but it also requires protection of the encryption keys. One answer is sealing of data, such as keys, so that it can only be used by authorized agents. But again, this raises the question of who to trust and how to prevent untrusted entities from gaining access.

---

[1]Example from the US Federal Bureau of Investigation (FBI), November 2011, `http://www.fbi.gov/news/stories/2011/november/malware_110911`.

Data-in-use refers to the data being manipulated by the application. Applications typically work on unencrypted data, so an attacker gaining access to that data circumvents any transport or storage protections. These attacks come from many different directions and target various components and operations. For example:

- *Frontal attack*: A direct attack on a system operation, generally by modifying or corrupting the system code or tricking the system.

- *Flanking*: *Reset attacks* have proven effective. This is where an attacker forces a reset after it has manipulated the BIOS to boot malicious software, which then inspects secrets and other privileged information that remain in memory.

- *Spying*: *Root kits* are an example of where an attacker causes the platform to boot malicious code that uses the platform's virtualization capabilities to then load the expected operating system in a false virtual environment. The system software is unaware that it is in a virtual environment and the root kit is now in control of the platform and has access to everything that the system places in memory.

A successful defense not only requires mechanisms to protect data, but also the means to detect changes and establish trust in the platform.

What Is Trust? How Can Hardware Help?

For most people, *trust* means that you have faith in someone or something to do the right thing. A broader definition would be "faith in someone or something to do something consistently." For instance, one might say that they "trust" that a computer virus will do harm—but they don't "trust" the virus. Generally, we trust the operating system to protect data and system resources, but we don't trust an operating system that has been infected with a virus or influenced by other malicious code. The challenge is to tell the difference.

Can we trust the system to determine if it is trustworthy? If you were to ask anyone if they can be trusted, they will likely respond "yes"—especially criminals. The same holds true for software, especially malicious software. To trust software, we need the ability to verify it in a way such that any change to the software changes its credential. For instance, if an operating system can prove that it is an authentic version and has not been modified, it deserves more trust than one that cannot. In fact, knowing that software has been modified is also valuable—because it allows corrective action such as quarantine and repair.

Thus we cannot depend on the software itself to detect if it has been modified (for example, infected with malicious code), because the malicious code might control or block the module that makes the trust decision. Thus we look to hardware to help make that determination.

The industry's leading security experts formed a nonprofit industry initiative known as the Trusted Computing Group[2] (TCG) to enhance trust and therefore security on computing platforms. The charter of the TCG is to develop industry standards for trusted computing building blocks and define their use for various platform types. Their efforts have produced a specification for a special security component (called a Trusted Platform Module, or TPM) and specifications for how to use that module in PCs and servers. These documents are available from the TCG web site (`www.trustedcomputinggroup.org/`). Several companies produce TPM chips that comply with these specifications, specifically for use on PCs and servers. The TPM chip is a very secure device that provides a number of security functions, and it is implemented in systems according to the TCG specifications by your favorite server manufacturers.

---

[2]`http://www.trustedcomputinggroup.org/`

A TPM chip is also one of the base components of Intel TXT, and provides the means to securely measure software components such as firmware, platform configuration, boot code, boot configuration, system code, system settings, and so on, to form a set of credentials for the platform components and system software. It also provides for accurately using those measurements as proof of trust and the ability to protect those measurements.

The measurement process for Intel TXT starts with hardware (that is, microcode designed into the Intel processor) and uses hardware (special chipset registers) to start the measurement process and store the measurements in the Trusted Platform Module chip in a way that cannot be spoofed by software.

What Is Intel® Trusted Execution Technology?

Intel TXT uses a combination of hardware, firmware, and software, and is built on and fully compliant with the Trusted Computing Group PC Client and Server specifications.

In general, Intel TXT is:

- A collection of security features.

- A means to verify that those features are in use.

- The means to securely measure and attest to system configuration and system code.

- A means to set policies to establish a trust level based on those measurements.
  Based on those policies, it is a means to:

  - Invoke enhanced capabilities (secure mode) for systems that meet that policy.

  - Prevent a system that fails the policy from entering the secure mode.

  - Determine if the system has entered the secure mode environment.

- The means for a trusted OS (that is, the system operating in the secure mode environment) to provide additional security features.

The ultimate goal of Intel TXT is to provide a more secure and hardened computing environment, but it is not a means to an end. Rather it is a tool for achieving higher levels of trust, and that trust does not come from simply enabling Intel TXT. The platform owner (e.g., datacenter IT manager) plays a key role in establishing what trust means, and Intel TXT provides the flexibility so that the system administrator can create a trust policy to match the requirements of the datacenter. Servers that implement Intel TXT can demonstrate (attest) that they comply with a specific trust policy, and thus can be used to form pools of trusted servers based on the established trust policy. Servers without Intel TXT and those that don't meet the trust policy can be excluded from the trusted pools. With the right policies in place, the datacenter can provide trusted pools of servers, allowing service clients to create "*use policies*" depending on the trust level. One example of this is the ability to confine critical applications (such as e-commerce services processing credit card information) to run only within a trusted pool. This has many applications for both private and public cloud providers, as well as their clients.

Before one can create a trust policy, it is important to understand what Intel TXT does and does not do. To put it in perspective, if we look at a bank's security, we find multiple security methods in use (locks on the doors, bars on the windows, a security alarm system, a surveillance system, a vault, armed guards, and so on). This is *defense in depth* and implies that no one method can do it all and that various methods come into play at different times (for example, doors and vaults tend to be unlocked and portions of the security alarm system are disabled during banking hours when armed guards are present). Of particular interest is to note that some of the methods are to prevent intrusion and others are just to detect and report it. The same is true for computer security; knowing when a breach has occurred is very important—just as a bank manager would not open the vault until he knows the bank is secure, Intel TXT can be configured to only allow the OS to launch if it knows the platform and system software are secure and trusted (as defined by the datacenter's policy). This *secure launch* allows the software to operate as a trusted OS, but only after validating that the platform configuration and system software meet the datacenter's policy.

So how do we define *secure* in this context? The short answer is to make sure that the system software is using all of the protection afforded by the processor and chipset architectures.

And how do we define *trusted?* The answer requires a means to measure the platform and the software. For servers, Intel TXT does that by incorporating two TCG concepts—a *static chain of trust* and a *dynamic chain of trust*, as illustrated in Figure 1-1. The static chain of trust measures the platform configuration, and the dynamic chain of trust measures the system software, software configuration, and software policies.

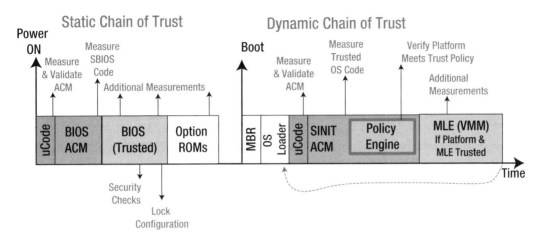

Figure 1-1. *Intel® TXT launch timeline with static and dynamic chain of trust*

Static Chain of Trust

The static chain of trust measurements start when the platform powers on. It starts with microcode that is embedded in the processor measuring an *authenticated code module* (ACM) provided by Intel. The ACM is a signed module (whose signature and integrity is authenticated by microcode) that performs special security functions. The ACM measures a portion of the BIOS code. That code then measures the remainder of BIOS code and configuration. Note that BIOS code does not execute until after it has been measured. These measurements are stored in special *platform configuration registers* (PCRs) inside a TPM (remember that the TPM is a very secure hardware device specified by the TCG). Different PCRs hold different launch component measurements (as specified by the TCG). During this process, the BIOS is required to turn on certain security features, and then call a function in the ACM that performs a security check. Before the BIOS executes any additional code, such as option ROMs on third-party adapters, it must lock the platform configuration by calling the ACM again, which performs additional security checks, and then locks certain platform and processor registers. The BIOS also measures the Master Boot Record (MBR) and the OS Loader when it boots the operating system.

The main takeaways are that measurements are started by hardware, measurements are protected from tampering by the TPM, and code is measured before it is executed.

These "static" measurements are done only once, each time the platform powers on. These measurements are referred to as *platform configuration* measurements.

Dynamic Chain of Trust

The dynamic chain of trust starts on request by the operating system (OS) via a special processor instruction, which measures and verifies another ACM (the SINIT ACM), which will oversee the secure launch. The SINIT ACM performs additional checks, which include making sure the BIOS passed its security checks and has locked the platform configuration. The ACM then measures the OS (actually a portion of the OS referred to as the *trusted OS*) and invokes a *launch control policy* (LCP) engine that will determine if the platform configuration and OS will be trusted (as defined by the policy set by the system administrator).

A *trusted OS* (a term used by the TCG for system code that invoked and passed the secure launch process—proving it meets the launch control policy) is allowed access to additional (privileged) security functions, including using additional PCRs. The trusted OS can measure such things as additional code, data, and configuration into those PCRs, and use the content of any of the PCRs to make trust decisions and seal/unseal data. Applications (both on and off the platform) can also use those measurements to make trust decisions.

Virtualization

Intel TXT works equally well for both virtualized and nonvirtualized platforms. In the course of bringing Intel TXT to market, the feedback has been quite strong that the primary and most compelling usage model for Intel TXT on servers is with virtualized and cloud-based server systems. This is generally because it addresses some of the key challenges introduced by moving to shared infrastructures. Specifically, it provides the ability to better control applications (in the form of virtual machines) and migration of applications among available platforms (the cloud) based on host trustworthiness. In other words, high availability and optimum utilization is achieved by migrating applications to available servers while still maintaining a trusted environment.

The term *OS* for a server platform can be confusing because of the existence of multiple operating systems on a virtualized host platform. This book uses the term *host OS* to refer to a hypervisor, virtual machine monitor (VMM), or in the case of a nonvirtualized platform, the traditional bare-metal operating system or any other application or utility that boots first. In any case, the host OS is the first system control program to boot. This is in contrast to an OS instantiated in a virtual machine (VM), which will be referred to as a *guest OS*. Furthermore, a trusted OS is a host OS that has successfully performed a *secure launch*. As a side note, while it is possible for the host OS to provide the same type of secure launch to its guest operating systems, that capability is outside the scope of the current version of Intel TXT and not discussed in this book.

OK, that last paragraph can be a little hard to read. So let's try these definitions:

- *OS*: The system software that manages platform resources and schedules applications. This includes

  - A hypervisor or virtual machine monitor that manages the *virtual machines.*

  - An OS that executes in a VM (i.e., the guest OS).

  - An OS executing on a nonvirtualized platform.

- *Host OS*: An OS that is not executing in a virtual machine, which can perform a secure launch, and thus can be measured by hardware (i.e., Intel TXT).

- *Guest OS*: An OS that is executing in a virtual machine, which is not measured by hardware.

- *Trusted OS*: A host OS that has performed a measured launch and passed the datacenter policy.

Measured Launch Environment

Because *trust* is a subjective term, Intel refers to the trusted OS as the *measured launch environment* (MLE), because Intel TXT certifies the measurement of the trusted OS (not its trust) and enforces the platform owner's policy—that is, it has measured the OS and platform configuration and verified that they meet the platform owner's launch policy. The measurements (i.e., the values in the PCRs) can be used by any entity to make a trust decision. For example, the platform owner can specify multiple OS measurements and platform configurations that will pass its launch policy, but an application can be more restrictive and trust only a subset. As we will see later, this concept can be extended and is the basis of attestation, which will be explained in detail later in this book.

The host OS is allowed to enter and exit the measured launch environment without having to reboot the platform. To exit, the host OS simply invokes another special processor instruction that will reset the PCRs that were used to measure the launch and those that were set by the trusted OS. Of course, this action also curtails the host operating system's access to some of the additional security resources. Reentering the secure environment restarts the dynamic chain of the trust process, and thus recalculates the MLE measurements storing them in those PCRs, allowing a different trusted OS (or different configuration of the same OS) to execute with its own set of trust credentials.

Finding Value in Trust

One of the nice things about Intel TXT is that its value can be appreciated by a number of different entities for various purposes. Some of these values have already been realized and there are many more to come.

Cloud Computing

Looking at a typical cloud management model, as illustrated in Figure 1-2, the cloud service provider maintains a pool of application servers, which hosts various applications provided by the cloud service clients. These applications are scheduled to run at times and locations to meet both provider and client polices.

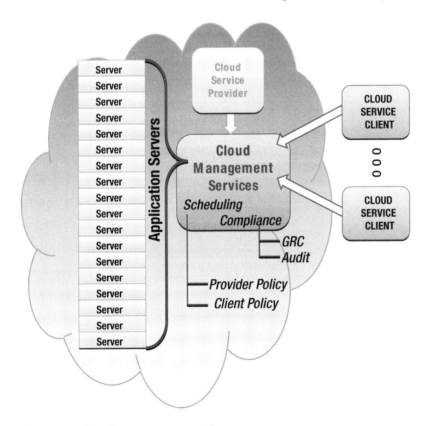

Figure 1-2. *Cloud management model*

The service provider must be able to demonstrate that the cloud meets governing regulations, and provide an audit trail to assure the client that all client and government requirements have been meet.

Because Intel TXT provides measurements of platform configurations and operating systems, adding Intel TXT to the picture allows the trust status of the application servers to enter into the equation. It allows both the service provider and the service client the ability to establish trust policies based on Intel TXT measurements and to identify servers that meet those polices, as illustrated in Figure 1-3.

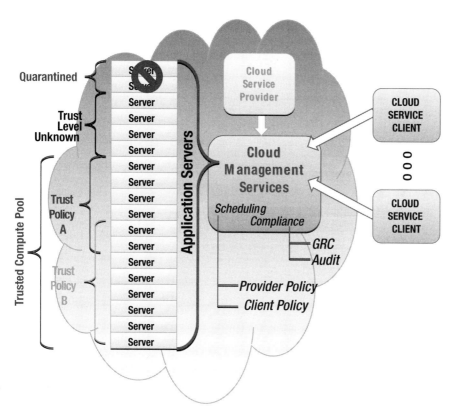

Figure 1-3. *Cloud management trust model*

Up till now, we have talked about measuring components, but the measurements themselves don't prove anything, or do they? Actually, it is the combination of the components that are measured, how the measurements are made, how the measurements are stored, and how the measurements are accessed that provides the basis for attestation.

Attestation: The Founding Principle

Furthering our discussion of how a bank uses multiple security concepts, let's focus on the banking transaction. Before executing a transaction, bank tellers require proof of the customer's identity. In the United States, that would typically be a driver's license or some other government-issued identification. State-issued driver's licenses and IDs have evolved over the years. In 1960, a license was simply a piece of paper printed with the state seal and folded in half to about the size of a business card. Personal information such as date of birth, height, weight, color of eyes, and hair color were typed in the respective boxes on that form by the issuing agency. Needless to say, it was fairly easy to modify, and thus subject to abuse. To reduce misuse and fraud, states started laminating each license with a photograph, thus making it harder to alter the data, and the photograph provided better identification. Of course, this assumes that the state issues the license to the right person. After the 9/11 attack, the US federal government placed more requirements on states—both on how the ID is created (including holographic images and special watermarks) and how the state validates the identity of the person being issued the license.

Just as a bank teller has to be able to verify the customer's identity, software needs a means to identify its environment. A driver's license is simply a certificate of attestation, and the same principles apply to validating software. One way to look at it is that the description on a license along with the photograph constitutes measurements of the person. That certificate also identifies who issued the certificate, and has features used to detect if it has been altered.

For Intel TXT, *attestation* is the ability to securely verify a set of component measurements. It is the founding principal for Intel TXT and accomplished by performing a cryptographic hash of each component. These components include BIOS code, BIOS configuration settings, I/O adapter option ROM code, I/O adapter configuration, MBR, bootstrap code, boot settings, ACM code, trust policies, OS code, OS configuration, and anything else that the OS wishes to measure. By measuring components using a cryptographic hash, corrupted components are easily detected via a change in their measurements.

But attestation involves more than just making the measurements. Those measurements constitute a certificate, and Intel TXT has to guarantee the following:

- The certificate comes from a trusted source

- The certificate is accurate

- The certificate has not been modified (at the source or in transit)

Value to System Software

You might ask why you need Intel TXT if you already trust the OS, since the processors and chipsets already provide a number of security features that the OS uses to protect itself against attacks, and you have installed virus protection and other security software. The first realization comes from the ability for the OS to use those functions, as well as load additional security software only after the OS loads. So what happens when the OS is not running? What about attacks against the relatively unprotected BIOS and the pre-boot environment? The following are some of the benefits that Intel TXT provides:

- Protection against reset attacks

- Protection against root kits

- Sealing data

- The ability to provide more secure services to VMs and applications

- System credentials

■ **Note**   Processors and chipsets provide a number of security features that an OS uses to protect itself from unintentional or malicious modification while it is running. Intel TXT extends that protection to when the OS is not running. That is, the OS has to start out uncorrupted for it to remain uncorrupted, and Intel TXT helps prove that the OS starts up uncorrupted.

Intel TXT makes it possible to detect unauthorized changes to BIOS and BIOS configuration, changes to the boot sequence, and changes to the OS and OS configuration. More important is that it provides an attestation mechanism that can be used by any entity that wishes to make a trust decision.

Cloud Service Provider/Cloud Service Client

Intel TXT's attestation opens up a whole new world of possibilities that can be realized by both local and remote entities. In addition to securely measuring and maintaining platform/OS measurements, Intel TXT provides the means to securely convey those measurements to external entities. Intel TXT also provides the means to determine if a platform is operating in the secure mode and for determining the policy for allowing secure mode. The datacenter sets the bar establishing the minimum trust level by setting the launch policy. Later, we take a close look at just what that means and how it is done, and discuss considerations in selecting a policy.

Management software can use this to provide capabilities such as:

- The ability to quarantine platforms with unauthorized modifications (that is, platforms that don't match "known good" configurations).

- Trusted compute pools and trust policy–based migration.

- Additional trust and security control metrics such as geo-tagging.

- Enhanced audit trail and compliance support.

Figure 1-3 illustrates how platforms can be categorized based on Intel TXT measurements. A trusted compute pool consists of those servers that have demonstrated that they have a known good configuration. This excludes those with an unknown trust level (those that don't support Intel TXT or don't have it enabled) and, of course, those that fail the Intel TXT launch control policy. The trusted compute pool can be further categorized into pools of trust based on various trust policies set by the service provider and service client.

As we continue to unravel the mysteries of Intel TXT, we will discover that the platform provides for 24 different secure measurements. Some are defined for specific purposes and others allow innovation. If one of the measurements included a geographic location identifier (geo-tag), policies could then limit applications to specified countries, states, or regions. This is especially important because a growing number of privacy laws and other governmental regulations stipulate controls and protections that vary depending on location or restrict data to certain geographical boundaries.

These capabilities are valuable for both public and private clouds. Even within a private cloud, different workloads have different security requirements—just as different workloads are assigned to different classes of servers in a traditional nonvirtualized datacenter. The ability to prove trust and maintain trust levels allows the cloud to host more restrictive applications, such as a finance or human resources department workloads that would no longer need separate compute facilities. These capabilities can give public cloud service providers the ability to enforce and charge according to the security level required. They give the public cloud service clients the tools to specify required trust levels and geographical boundaries, as well as the means to validate compliance to those requirements.

Before we discuss these capabilities—and they will be covered in more depth in subsequent chapters—we need to understand more about how Intel TXT works and from where the trust comes. As we progress through this book, we will answer the following questions:

- How does Intel TXT provide attestation, and what makes it so powerful?

- How does the system administrator enable it?

- How does the datacenter take advantage of it?

- How does system software use it?

- How do others make use of it?

Then we will take a closer look at attestation and how it is currently used. To get a glimpse of the future, we will also discuss concepts that are being evaluated and prototyped.

What Intel TXT Does *Not* Do

Intel TXT does not measure trust, nor does it define levels of trust. These are subjective terms whose definitions will change over time. Rather, Intel TXT allows the datacenter/cloud service provider, cloud service client, OS, and other entities to make their own trust decisions with a new set of robust credentials. These trust decisions can be, but do not have to be, based solely on Intel TXT. In fact, since *defense in depth* refers to using multiple methods to protect your assets, Intel TXT assumes that other security mechanisms exist, new technologies will emerge, and together they will provide greater coverage. Intel TXT is flexible enough that it can be used to help verify proper utilization of other methods and their policies.

Intel TXT does not monitor runtime configuration. It only performs measurements at specific events, such as *Power On*, and upon request by the host OS to do a secure launch. Therefore, it does not degrade performance since it does not steal cycles from the operating system or applications running on the platform, nor does it consume memory bandwidth and other operational resources after the secure launch.

Currently, Intel TXT only measures the host OS or VMM and does not provide for secure measurements of a guest OS or its applications. This is a topic of discussion and interest throughout the industry, and it would be very surprising if this capability is not added in the future.

Enhancements for Servers

As mentioned at the beginning, Intel TXT was first developed for client platforms (desktop and mobile). So is it the same technology? There are some differences, primarily because servers are more complex than client machines. One of the most prominent differences is the set of server features known as Reliability, Availability, and Serviceability (RAS). The complexity of server RAS features such as memory mirroring, memory sparing, and error handling require capabilities that are very platform-specific, and thus must be performed by platform-specific code. This code must be trusted; in particular, the BIOS code that executes after a platform reset (to mitigate the reset attack) and the System Management Module (SMM) code, which may need to change memory configuration and/or platform configuration while the system is in operation.

This changes what the TCG refers to as the TCB (Trusted Computing Base), which, by definition, is the minimum amount of code that needs to be trusted for a platform. For server platforms, the TCB includes the processor microcode and the ACM, whose signature and integrity are checked before the ACM is allowed to execute. It must also include the BIOS (or at least a portion of the BIOS).

Including BIOS in the TCB

For client platforms, the BIOS does not need to be trusted to clear memory in defense of a reset attack, because memory cleaning is performed by the ACM before allowing the BIOS to access the memory. This is not possible for servers given the complexity of server memory configurations and RAS features. Thus in response to (or to detect) a reset attack, BIOS code integrity must be verified before the BIOS can be trusted to clean secrets from memory. Typically, this is transparent to the OS and end user, but it does have implications on how BIOS upgrades occur. For instance, upgrading BIOS causes its measurement to change, and if there is a reset attack after a BIOS update, the BIOS would not be trusted. To overcome this problem, Intel TXT allows for a signed BIOS policy that allows the ACM to validate that the BIOS is still trusted using signature verification.

Processor-Based CRTM

Because the BIOS must be trusted to clear memory after a reset attack, a trust decision must be made before BIOS is allowed to execute. This means that the BIOS has to be measured (or at least the portion of it that clears the memory) and that measurement has to be verified. This adds complexity to the BIOS because it must now provide a table that identifies the code that will be executed to clear memory and also specify the type of policy that the hardware uses to validate that code. Unless the verification fails, this will be transparent to the user and the software.

Trusting the SMM

Client platforms with Intel TXT can use an SMI Transfer Monitor (STM) to prevent SMM code from corrupting the platform configuration. The complexity of servers and the need for the SMM to handle RAS concepts such as memory and processor hot plug (a common term for the removal or replacement of these components while a server is operating) require that the SMM code be inside the trust domain. This means that the SMM code has to be measured as part of the BIOS code measurement, and thus included in the trust decision to allow the OS to perform a secure launch. Again, this is transparent to the OS and the end user, but it will show up in the logs that describe what is included in the BIOS measurement.

Other Differences

As alluded to previously, the complexity of Intel TXT increases on servers because of the server architecture complexity. This includes multiple processor sockets, enhanced I/O, base board management, and so on. Whereas these features make it harder on the BIOS developer, they tend to be transparent to the end user and the software using Intel TXT.

Impact of the Differences

The bottom line is that any operating system that functions with the client version of Intel TXT also functions with the server version. The platform credentials will be different, but each platform type will have a different measurement anyway. The OS measurements are performed exactly the same way for client and server platforms.

Even though the usage models differ greatly between client and server platforms, their Intel TXT behaviors have intentionally been kept consistent. This allows client operating systems to be used on server platforms and server operating systems to be used on client platforms—where this would be desirable.

Because the OS launches exactly the same and the integrity of the measurements does not change, applications using Intel TXT attestation work the same.

Roles and Responsibilities

So you have an Intel TXT-enabled platform—now what? What are your responsibilities? What precautions do you need to take? What about system software? What else is needed? Let's take a quick look at what is expected of all of the players. These roles and responsibilities will be explored in greater detail in subsequent chapters of this book.

OEM

The OEM puts together all of the components, and then packages them into an Intel TXT-capable platform. This design is thoroughly tested to assure that the platform complies with Intel TXT requirements and is able to perform a secure launch. The OEM often does the initial provisioning of the TPM before the platform ships. With the exception of occasional BIOS updates, the OEM's job is done once the platform leaves the factory.

Platform Owner

The platform arrives with Intel TXT and the TPM disabled. This is to prevent rogue software from taking over and setting its own trust policies, or launching a denial of service attack by consuming all of the TPM resources. What needs to be done next depends on the host OS that you are installing.

Before installing an Intel TXT–enabled OS, you have to enable the TPM and Intel TXT via the BIOS setup menus. Depending on the OS, you may need to establish TPM ownership and set the launch control policy (or the OS might do that for you). We will discuss how to do this later, as well as discuss tradeoffs for selecting a launch control policy.

Host Operating System

Operating system installation detects if a TPM is enabled and whether TPM ownership has been established. As mentioned earlier, the OS might require exclusive TPM ownership, and thus the OS performs the TPM "take ownership" operation itself, as well as sets the launch control policy. If so, it will do this as part of the install process on first boot. For this case, the OS provides the utilities for the platform owner to modify the policy.

Each time the host OS boots, it detects if Intel TXT is enabled, and if so, performs a secure launch. As a trusted OS, it continues measuring system code, configuration, and other entities into the platform configuration registers reserved for the OS. The host OS maintains a log that indicates what has been measured into each register.

The host OS provides remote access to certain TPM resources (such as platform configuration registers) and associated logs. This allows external management applications to make trust-based decisions using the Intel TXT measurements.

Other Software

As we progress through this book, we will see the various roles that are played by third-party software. We will discuss attestation services and trust authorities, and their importance to both the cloud service provider and the cloud service client.

There are no hard and fast rules for using Intel TXT attestation. Typically, third-party software uses Intel TXT measurements in the platform configuration registers to verify which host OS is in control (and which version). Knowing which host OS then provides insight into what the trusted OS has measured into the platform configuration registers reserved for the trusted OS.

For example, one application could use certain PCRs to verify which OS is in control and its version. Based on that information, another application could verify OS-specific values, such as geographic location measured into one of the platform configuration registers used by that OS. Other applications can use that information to make trust-based policy decisions.

■ ■ ■

CHAPTER 2

Fundamental Principles of Intel® TXT

The first step to more secure computing is improved hardware. So before we discuss how to use the technology, let's define what constitutes an Intel® TXT–capable platform and the underlying principles behind the technology. We will take a look at the unique components, how they work together, and what they do to produce a more secure environment.

What You Need: Definition of an Intel® TXT–Capable System

Intel TXT relies on a set of enhanced hardware, software, and firmware components designed to protect sensitive information from software-based attacks. These components are illustrated in Figure 2-1 and Figure 2-2.

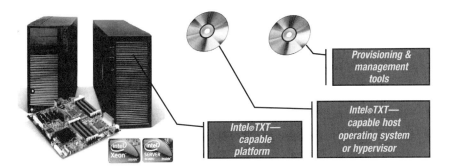

Figure 2-1. *Intel® TXT-capable system*

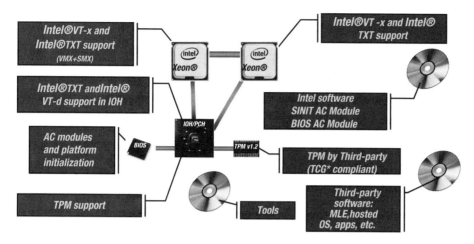

Figure 2-2. *Intel TXT platform components*

As illustrated in Figure 2-1, it takes more than just an Intel TXT–capable platform. An Intel TXT–capable platform provides the foundation; however, to get the full value from this technology one needs to install an Intel TXT–capable operating system. (Intel TXT–capable platform systems will be discussed shortly.) In addition, provisioning tools and other management software may be needed to tune Intel TXT operation to meet datacenter policy, as well as enable service clients to benefit from it. For now, let's focus on the platform and answer the question: What makes Intel TXT different and why?

Intel® TXT–Capable Platform

The platform components are illustrated in Figure 2-2, but don't worry, it is the platform manufacturer who is responsible for integrating and testing these components. This means that by the time a platform reaches the datacenter, it is Intel TXT–capable (or it is not). Intel TXT–ready server platforms did not start shipping until early 2010, so older platforms are not Intel TXT–capable. As of 2012, most major manufacturers offer Intel TXT–capable server platforms. It should be pointed out that some manufacturers have designed server platforms that can be upgraded to being Intel TXT–capable via a BIOS upgrade and/or a plug-in module. So check with your platform vendor to find out if existing platforms are Intel TXT–capable.

As we review the various components of Intel TXT, these topics may seem disjointed or incomplete, but as the chapter progresses, it will become apparent just how they all work together.

Intel TXT Platform Components

The recipe for a platform that is able to support Intel TXT includes the following ingredients specifically designed for Intel TXT.

Processor

All Intel IA32 server processors, beginning with the Intel® Xeon® 5600 series, (codenamed Westmere[1]) support Intel TXT. This support includes a new security instruction (GETSEC, part of the Safer Mode Extensions known as SMX). This new instruction performs multiple security functions (referred to as *leaves*). Two of the leaf functions

---

[1]Released in the first quarter of 2010.

(GETSEC[ENTERACCS] and GETSEC[SENTER]) provide the ability to securely validate *authenticated code modules* (ACMs) and (if valid) invoke that authenticated code using a very secure area within the processor that is protected from external influence (see the "Authenticated Code Modules" section). All processors that support Intel TXT also support Intel® Virtualization Technology (i.e., VMX instructions and an enhanced architecture for increased isolation and protection). There is no limit on the number of processors, thus Intel TXT is found on UP, DP, and MP platforms. Actually, the number of processor cores is limited to a 32-bit value (4,294,967,295 maximum value), but for all practical purposes, this is not a limiting factor.

Chipset

Intel chipsets designed to work with Intel Xeon 5600 series and later processors include:

- special TXT registers
- an enhanced architecture
- controlled access to the Trusted Platform Module (TPM)

It is the chipset that enforces TPM locality (defined later) and enforces different access rights to the TXT registers, depending on the security level of the entity attempting to access the TXT registers. Other chipset manufactures can also build chipsets that implement Intel TXT (they would provide their own ACMs). Unless otherwise noted, we will be discussing Intel chipsets and ACMs.

Trusted Platform Module (TPM)

Intel TXT makes extensive use of the *Trusted Platform Module* (TPM), a component defined by the Trusted Computing Group[2] (TCG). The TPM provides a number of security features (more on this in the section titled "The Role of the Trusted Platform Module (TPM)." In particular, the TPM provides a secure repository for measurements and the mechanisms to make use of those measurements. A system makes use of the measurements for both reporting and evaluating the current platform configuration and for providing long-term protection of sensitive information.

BIOS

The platform BIOS is specially designed to configure the platform for secure mode operation. BIOS plays a significant role, whose duties include:

- Supplying the ACMs. ACMs are created by the chipset vendor and provided to the BIOS developer to be included as part of the BIOS image.
- Configuring the platform for Intel TXT operation.
- Performing a security check and registering with the ACM.
- Locking the platform's configuration using the processor's GETSEC security instruction.

Once locked, BIOS and other firmware can no longer modify the configuration. BIOS performs this locking before executing any third-party code such as option ROMS on add-in cards.

---

[2]The Trusted Computing Group (TCG) is a not-for-profit organization dedicated to advancing computer security whose goals are to develop, define, and promote open industry standards for trusted computing building blocks and software interfaces (www.TrustedComputingGroup.org).

Authenticated Code Module (ACM)

An *authenticated code module* is a piece of code provided by the chipset manufacturer. This module is signed by the manufacturer and executes at one of the highest security levels within a special secure memory internal to the processor. Most Intel-based platforms use Intel chipsets, thus the ACMs for those platforms are created by and signed by Intel.

Each ACM is designed to work with a specific chipset, and thus is matched to the chipset. ACMs are invoked using the processor GETSEC instruction. There are two types of ACMs: BIOS ACM and SINIT ACM. The BIOS ACM measures the BIOS and performs a number of BIOS-based security functions. The SINIT ACM is used to perform a secure launch of the system software (operating system). SINIT is an acronym for Secure Initialization because it initializes the platform so the OS can enter the secure mode of operation.

The BIOS image contains both the BIOS ACM and the SINIT ACM; however, the OS may choose to supply a more recent version of the SINIT ACM when it does a secure launch.

As we will see later, the ACM is the core root of trusted measurements, and as such, it operates at the highest security level and must be protected against all forms of attack. Because of this, the following extra precautions are taken to verify and protect the ACM.

- The processor's microcode performs a number of security checks on the ACM before allowing the ACM to execute:

  - ACM must match the chipset

  - ACM version must not have been revoked

  - ACM must be signed

  - Signature must be valid

- Before the processor makes these checks, it copies the ACM into protected memory inside the processor, so that the ACM code cannot be modified after it is validated.

- A checksum of the public signing key is hardcoded in the chipset and used to verify that the ACM was signed with the proper signing key. Each chipset generation uses a different signing key. Thus, only someone who has the private key can create an ACM. The private keys are very well guarded and only a few very trusted Intel people have access to the private keys.

- The signature uses cryptography to validate that the ACM has not been altered.

Thus the GETSEC instruction will only execute the ACM if the ACM was signed with the correct key, matches the chipset, and has not been modified.

The Role of the Trusted Platform Module (TPM)

It is hard to talk about Intel TXT without referring to the TPM. The TPM is an important component specified by the Trusted Computing Group (www.trustedcomputinggroup.org) expressly for improving security. We really applaud the TCG for defining such an ingenious device. The TPM specification is in three volumes (four, if you count the compliance volume) and there are books just on the TPM. Luckily for us, we don't have to go into great detail. However, an understanding of the key features will provide a better appreciation of how Intel TXT provides secure measurements.

Currently, platforms incorporate TPMs adhering to version 1.2 of the TCG TPM specification. Version 2.0, which is expected to be released late 2013. It provides the same functionality plus includes enhanced features, capabilities, and capacities.

The primary security functions provided by the TPM are illustrated in Figure 2-3.

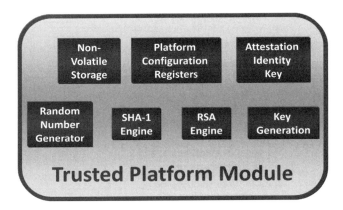

Figure 2-3. *Trusted Platform Module*

TPM Interface

The TPM interface is simple, making it easier to defend. The TPM connects to the chipset by the Low Pin Count (LPC) bus[3] and is only accessed via memory mapped I/O (MMIO) registers protected by the chipset. This means that I/O devices cannot access the TPM at all and the OS can easily control which processes have access to the TPM. In addition, the TPM enforces additional protections and access rights.

Localities

The TPM has different privileged levels called *localities*. Each locality is accessed by a different 4K page allowing both hardware and software to control access to each locality. The chipset controls which localities are active (that is, whether a read or write to that page will be ignored) and system software can control which processes have access to those pages via normal memory management and paging functions. There are five localities (0 through 4) and Intel TXT uses the localities as shown in Table 2-1.

Table 2-1. *TPM Locality*

Locality	Access
0	Always open for general use.
1	Operating system (not used as part of TXT).
2	System software (OS) in secure mode. Only after the OS has successfully performed a secure launch. The OS may close this access at any time.
3	ACMs. Only an ACM that has been invoked by the GETSEC instruction has access to locality 3.
4	Hardware. Only the processor executing its microcode has Locality 4 access.

Note that these localities are not hierarchical. Thus, locality 4 is not a super-user and does not automatically have access to keys, data, and resources available to other localities. Later, we will look at the use of localities for protection of keys and data.

---

[3]Future TPMs may use the Serial Peripheral Interface (SPI) bus, but the principles are the same.

Control Protocol

The interface to the TPM is message based. That is, an entity creates a request message and sends it to the TPM (via a locality page) and then reads the response message (via the locality page). The protocol allows the entity (using messages) to set up a secure session. Sessions allow the user to encrypt the message content, but more importantly, the means to authenticate authorization.

Messages that require authorization contain one or more authorization fields, called *HMAC keys*. HMAC stands for Hash Method of Authentication. The HMAC key is calculated as the hash of the message, a nonce (number used once), and the authorization value. The nonce and authorization values are not part of the message, and thus must be known by both parties.

The HMAC in a request demonstrates that the caller knows the authorization value and is therefore authorized to issue the TPM command. In the response, the HMAC value authenticates that the response came from the TPM and has not been modified during transport.

The protocol is as follows. Each message in a session uses a different set of random numbers (nonces) to generate the HMAC key(s). The requester provides the odd nonce that the TPM uses to calculate the HMAC value in its reply and the reply contains the even nonce that the requester uses to calculate the HMAC value in its next request. This prevents *replay attacks* and *man-in-the-middle attacks* because the HMAC value changes for any change in the message. Even the exact same command will have a different HMAC value each time it is issued (because the nonce is different).

Let's look at an example.

1. The caller sets up a session by sending a start session command to the TPM and the TPM responds with a session handle and the TPM's nonce.

2. The caller creates a command that requires authorization (that is, requires that the caller prove that the caller knows the password associated with the object of the command). To do this, the caller creates a cryptographic hash of the command, plus the nonce provided by the TPM, plus the password.

3. The caller sends the command, the caller's nonce, and the hash digest to the TPM. Note that the password is not sent.

4. The TPM then performs the same hash except using the real password of the object. If that hash digest matches the digest in the command message, then the TPM concludes that the caller knows the password, and that the command has not been altered in transport.

5. In the response, the TPM provides a new TPM-nonce that the caller uses in the next command. The response also contains the hash digest of the response parameters, plus the odd nonce from the request message, plus the password.

Note that the caller could have also set up a session so that the command parameters and response parameters were encrypted.

The bottom line is that the TPM is a very hardened device that protects its resources and requires specific access authorization that is protected from tampering.

Random Number Generator (RNG)

Random numbers are used in safeguarding communication between a requesting entity and the TPM, especially when that entity is remote to the platform. Unlike a pseudo RNG that software applications use, the TPM's random number generator is a true RNG and can provide entropy for other purposes. Thus, in addition to using random numbers to protect TPM transport, an entity can request a random number from the TPM for other purposes, such as encryption and securing external channels.

SHA-1 Engine

The TPM hashing algorithm is SHA-1 (pronounced *Shah-one*), which is a cryptographic hash function designed by the United States National Security Agency as a US Federal Information Processing Standard. SHA stands for *secure hash algorithm*. This hashing produces a 20-byte (160-bit) digest. The hash is used for various authorization and authentication processes. The TPM's SHA-1 engine is used internally to do the following:

- Authenticate request messages
- Authorize response messages
- Calculate the hash digest of code and data
- Extend PCR values
- Authenticate/authorize keys

For more information on SHA-1, see the "Cryptographic Hash Functions" section.

RSA Engine and Key Generation

The TPM uses the RSA asymmetric algorithm for digital signatures and for encryption. RSA stands for Ron Rivest, Adi Shamir, and Leonard Adleman, who published the algorithm for public-key cryptography in 1978. The key generator uses that algorithm to generate asymmetric keys (a public key and a private key). The private key is kept internal[4] to the TPM (thus only known to the TPM). The public key) is used by an entity to encrypt data that can only be decrypted by someone with the private key (the TPM). The RSA engine uses the keys to encrypt and decode messages and data.

The "Cryptography" section provides details on how keys are generated and used.

Platform Configuration Registers (PCRs)

Pay attention. There will be a quiz later. Just joking, but PCRs are one of the two TPM features that are accessed as objects and the basis of attestation, as well as used in launch control policy. Thus, they play a key role.

The TPM provides special protected registers to store measurements. These registers are known as Platform Configuration Registers (PCRs). Each PCR has an inherent property of a cryptographic hash. That is, each PCR holds a 20-byte hash digest. Entities never write directly to a PCR, rather they "extend" a PCR's content. For the extend operation, the TPM takes the current value of the PCR, appends the value to be extended, performs SHA-1 hash on the combined value, and the resulting hash digest becomes the new PCR value. Therefore, each PCR holds a composite hash of all of the elements that have been measured to it. This means that PCRs cannot be spoofed—the only way for a PCR to have a specific value is if the exact same measurements are extended to it in the exact same order. Any variation results in a PCR value that is very different. This is a key concept that provides secure generation and protection of measurements.

Intel TXT uses TPMs that have 24 PCRs. Some PCRs are static, which means that their values are only reset when the system first powers on by the power-up-reset signal. Thus, measurements stored in those PCRs persist until the platform powers down and are used to hold the static chain of trust measurements. Other PCRs are dynamic, which means their value can be reset to their default values, but only via certain localities (as specified by the TCG). These are used for the dynamic chain of trust measurements. The PCRs that hold the dynamic chain of trust measurements can only be reset by the ACM.

---

[4]Because the TPM has limited internal storage, the key might be encrypted and stored external to the TPM as a blob. But the value of the key is not known externally.

Nonvolatile Storage

TPMs provide nonvolatile storage, that is, memory that is persistent across power cycles and has more security features than system memory. This nonvolatile random access memory (NVRAM) is the other TPM feature that is exposed externally as objects and plays an important role in creating and protecting the launch control policy set by the datacenter manager.

Compared to system memory, TPM NVRAM is very small, on the order of 2000 bytes, so it is a precious resource. NVRAM is allocated in small chunks and the entity that allocates a chunk of NVRAM specifies access rights for that data. To give you an idea of how flexible and powerful TPM NVRAM is, let's look at what needs to be specified to allocate TPM NVRAM:

- An index (an ID that identifies that chunk).

- The size of that chunk.

- Read access rights.

    - Specifies which localities are allowed to read the data.

    - Specifies if any PCRs must contain specific values in order to read the data. Data cannot be read if any of the selected PCRs do not contain their expected value.

- Write access rights.

    - Specifies which localities are allowed to write the data.

    - Specifies if any PCRs must contain specific values in order to write the data. Data cannot be written if any of the selected PCRs do not contain their expected value. The set of selected PCRs can be different than those selected for read access. Also, the expected PCR values can be different.

- Attributes/permissions. Can specify any of the following:

    Read

    - Temporal read lock. The value can be read until locked by a read of zero length; unlocked at the next power cycle.

    - What authorization is required to read; may specify:

        - None.

        - A specific authorization value (like a password) is required.

        - If physical presence assertion is required. Physical assertion typically means BIOS is performing the access.

    Write

    - Persistent Lock. The value can be locked for write access (by a write of zero length) and once locked can never be altered.

    - Temporal Write Lock. The value can be locked for write access (by a write of zero length), and once locked, cannot be altered until the next power cycle.

    - Write Once. The value can only be written once per power cycle/ unlocked at the next power cycle.

    - Whether partial writes are allowed.

- What authorization is required to write; may specify:

    - None (when PCRs or locality restrict write access).

    - A specific authorization value (like a password) is required.

    - If physical presence assertion is required.

As you can see, NVRAM capabilities are very flexible. To give an example, ACMs makes use of these capabilities to allocate a chunk of NVRAM that they use to save state and pass data between ACMs. The protection comes from specifying that only localities 3 and 4 can write to that index (since only the ACM and microcode can access the TPM using locality 3 or 4). We will see later that this allows the ACM to store the BIOS measurement and detect if BIOS code has changed from one boot to the next. Other indexes are used for setting launch control policy and they specify different attributes and access rights. The bottom line is that even though hardware and system software control who can access the TPM, it is the entity that allocates the chunk of NVRAM that determines under what conditions the data can be read and written, as well establishes if a password is required, and then specifies the password.

Attestation Identity Key (AIK)

The *Attestation Identity Key* (AIK) is a concept that allows a TPM to certify that keys and data originated from the TPM without revealing any platform-specific identity information. An entity (like a certification authority) can create an AIK. This causes the TPM to create an asymmetric key pair that it uses to sign keys created by the TPM or sign data reported by the TPM (such as PCR values). The root of the certificate can be traced back to the TPM vendor and verified that it is, in fact, a compliant TPM.

TPM Ownership and Access Enforcement

One last point to cover is the TPM enforcement. A TPM arrives at the platform manufacturer in an unlocked state to make it easy for the manufacturer to create NVRAM indexes. At this stage, the TPM does not enforce any access controls. The manufacturer provisions the TPM creating the indexes required by Intel TXT and then performs an OEM lock. The OEM lock protects those indexes so that their access policy cannot be changed. It also prevents anyone from creating an NVRAM index that falls in range of indexes reserved for the platform manufacturer.

When the platform arrives at the customer's datacenter, the TPM is disabled and inactivated to prevent rogue software from taking ownership and mounting a "Denial of Service" attack. Taking ownership is a process where an entity reads the TPMs Endorsement Key (EK) and uses it to encrypt a TPM Owner Authorization value (think of this authorization as the TPM owner's password) and then sends the encrypted password to the TPM in a "Take Ownership" command.

The TPM Owner Authorization value is typically a SHA-1 hash of a password or pass phrase and it is used to prove to the TPM that certain commands (such as allocating NVRAM) are authorized by the platform owner.

Prior to establishing TPM ownership, the TPM does not accept commands that allocate TPM resources, like allocating TPM NVRAM and creating keys. After establishing TPM ownership, those commands require owner authorization (that is, knowledge of the TPM owner's password).

Cryptography

Since not everyone is familiar with encryption standards, let's review some fundamental concepts.

- Encryption is the process of using an algorithm (called a cipher) to transform plaintext information to make it unreadable to anyone except those possessing a special key.

- Decryption is the reverse process, to make encrypted information readable again (that is, make it unencrypted by changing ciphertext back into plaintext).

- Encryption is used to protect data and for authentication (such as for a digital signature).

- There are two parts to encryption. The first is key creation and the second is the encryption/decryption process.

- There are two classes of encryption algorithms (symmetric and asymmetric).

Symmetric Encryption

Symmetric encryption is where the same key[5] used to encrypt the data is also used to decrypt it. Symmetric encryption is generally faster than asymmetric encryption. Its primary use is where the same entity is performing both the encryption and decryption of the data, such as for protecting data saved to disk. This is sometimes referred to as *one-party encryption* because the entity that encrypts the data can also decrypt the data.

Asymmetric Encryption

Asymmetric encryption is where a different key is used to decrypt the data than the key used to encrypt it. These two keys are referred to as the public key and the private key. It is not possible to derive the private key from the public key. The following are some use models:

- *Signing.* The private key is the encryption key. The signer uses it to encrypt a hash of the module being signed (known as the module's signature). The pubic decryption key is appended to the module being signed along with the encrypted signature. Other parties can verify that the module comes from the signer by verifying that the public key was issued by the signer—usually through a *certification authority* (CA). The module's integrity is then verified by calculating the hash of the module and comparing it to the modules signature decrypted with the public key.

- *Endorsement.* The private key is the decryption key. The public key is provided to another party that uses it to encrypt sensitive data (such as a password) that can only be decrypted by the first entity.

- *Secure transmission.* Uses two pairs of keys where the private keys are the decryption keys. Each end of a secure channel creates their own key pair and provides the other end of the channel with the public key, which is used to encrypt transmissions.

Private keys must be very guarded and are never passed in the clear. Public keys do not require protection because the knowledge of the public key does not reveal any secrets nor does it provide access to any privileged information.

Intel TXT supports PKCS[6] #1.5, a public standard for encryption that allows key sizes of 1024, 2048, or 3072 bits and recommends a minimum key size of 2048.

Cryptographic Hash Functions

A cryptographic hash is the result of performing a specific hash algorithm on a block of data. The purpose of the hash function (often called *hashing*) is to map a large/variable size block of data to a smaller fixed-length data set, referred to as a hash, hash digest, or digest. The SHA-1 algorithm maps any amount of data to a 20-byte hash digest while the SHA-256 algorithm maps any amount of data to a 32-byte hash digest.

---

[5]Sometimes one key is derived from the other, but the concept is still the same.
[6]PKCS stands for Public Key Cryptography Standards, which was published by RSA Data Security Inc., now a subsidiary of EMC Corporation.

Cryptographic hash functions are used for many purposes. Intel TXT uses it to detect changes in code, data, messages, configuration, or anything else that may be stored in memory—because any accidental or intentional change to what is being measured or verified will drastically change the hash value. The following are properties of a cryptographic hash:

- The digest is easy to compute.

- It is not reasonably possible to create a block of data that produces a given hash. We say "not reasonably possible" because given enough time, anything is possible. A 20-byte value has 2^{160} values. So do the math to figure out how long it would take to just generate 2^{160} values. Even using a million computers, it would take billions of billions of years.

- It is not reasonably possible to modify a block of data without changing its hash digest.

- It is not reasonably probable to find two different blocks of data with the same hash digest.

Therefore, it is reasonable to claim that a hash of an entity is a unique identifier of that entity and only that entity will have that hash value. There are many applications for cryptographic hash functions:

- *Digital signature*. The signer encrypts the hash of the module being signed. Other parties can verify that the module comes from the signer by verifying that the public key was issued by the signer, and then verify the module's integrity by calculating the hash of the module and comparing it to the modules signature decrypted with the public key.

- *Digital fingerprint*. A hash of a block of data differentiates that data from any other data. One use is when that block of data is code. Thus the hash of the code becomes a unique identifier. The same applies to a data file, configuration settings, and so on. We have already discussed how Intel TXT measures code, configuration, and other elements to TPM PCR registers.

- *Message authentication*. When both the sender and receiver have a secret authentication value (typically the hash of a password or passphrase). The sender of a message creates a hash of the message concatenated with the secret authentication value to produce an authentication key, and appends that key to the message. The recipient verifies that the sender knows the correct secret authentication value by performing the same hash calculation (using his copy of the secret authentication value) and comparing the result to the authentication key passed with the message. The secret authentication value is not sent in the message. If the sender used the wrong value or the message was modified in transit, the keys will not match, and thus the recipient rejects the message. Therefore, this is both authentication and authorization because the sender authorizes the message by using the secret authentication value and the recipient authenticates that the message came from an authorized source and was not modified in transit. This is the Hash Method of Authentication (HMAC) that we discussed as part of the TPM control protocol.

- *Checksums*. A hash digest of a block of data can easily be used to validate that the data has not been altered. An example is how Intel TXT verifies the launch control policy. Since the size of TPM NVRAM is limited, some of the policy is stored in flash or on disk. The hash measurement of the portion of the policy stored on disk is securely stored in the TPM NVRAM. Any change to the external policy data results in a mismatch of its hash measurement to the hash value stored in the TPM.

Why It Works and What It Does

Now that we have all of the pieces, let's put the puzzle together and discuss what Intel TXT does that is different from previous platform designs.

Key Concepts

Here are some of the key concepts of Intel TXT.

- Intel TXT provides for the following:
  - Secure measurement
  - Dynamic launch mechanisms via special instructions
  - Configuration locking
  - Sealing secrets
- Intel TXT helps detect and/or prevent software attacks such as:
  - Attempts to insert nontrusted VMM (rootkit hypervisor)
  - Reset attacks designed to compromise secrets in memory
  - BIOS and firmware update attacks

Measurements

A measurement is a cryptographic hash of code, data, or anything that can be loaded into memory (such as policies, configuration, keys, and passwords). The default hashing algorithm is SHA-1, which produces a 20-byte (160-bit) digest with the following properties:

- A single bit change in the entity being measured causes a majority of the bits in the hash digest to change. Thus any change to the entity being measured can be easily detected.

- The hash algorithm is not reciprocal—that is, the hash process cannot be reversed. Thus, it is impossible to reconstruct the measured entity from its hash digest. This is important when using the hash to authenticate passwords (that is, a password hash used to verify a password cannot be used to construct a valid password).

- The likelihood of any two entities (that are not identical) having the same measurement are astronomical (2^{160} is an enormously large number).

Intel TXT also supports SHA-256 for some measurements, but SHA-1 is the default for all measurements. And it is the only hashing algorithm supported by the TPM 1.2 family devices. Earlier, it was noted that there was a new specification for the TPM 2.0 family of devices on the horizon. These new devices will be able to support additional hashing and encryption algorithms.

Secure Measurements

Measuring code and configuration is not meaningful unless the measurements can be guaranteed to be authentic, accurate, and protected.

So what constitutes a "secure" measurement? The answer is twofold:

- The measurement is hardware rooted (hardware root of trust).

- The measurements are protected from tampering.

To understand *root of trust*, we need to define *chain of trust*. The chain of trust starts with a trusted component that measures the next component. That component then measures the next component, and so on until all components that need to be measured have been. The root of trust is the component that started the measurement chain.

For TXT, the root of trust is the processor. When the server boots, and before any BIOS code is permitted to execute, a special microcode built into the processor performs a validity check on the BIOS ACM and then measures the BIOS ACM before it is executed. The BIOS ACM then measures a portion of the BIOS referred to as *startup BIOS*. The startup BIOS then measures other portions of the BIOS code. This is important because the entity that starts the measurement chain and makes the first measurement establishes the accuracy of that measurement chain.

At this point, it should be obvious that the final value is not necessarily a single operation, but results from multiple measurements that need to be processed together to form a single result. This process is referred to as *extending*. It is the TPM that provides the protection from tampering. The TPM contains a set of Platform Configuration Registers (PCRs). These PCRs cannot be written but rather are extended. The phrase *extending a PCR* means hashing the existing PCR content with the new measurement to create the new PCR content. Thus, extending is the means to concatenate multiple measurements into a single result. It is the TPM itself that performs the extending operation, thus software only provides the measurement to be extended and identifies which PCR is to be extended. But not all software has access to the TPM and certain PCRs can only be extended from specific localities.

Since PCRs are extended (not written), even if malicious software was able to extend a PCR, the only impact is that the PCR would carry an invalid measurement—remember that one of the SHA-1 hash properties is that it is not possible to create a block of data that produces a given hash. Thus, it is not possible to extend a PCR to get a given result, except by measuring the exact same objects in the exact same order. Since one of the Intel TXT principles is not to execute code until it has been measured, we can conclude that the measurement already includes the malicious code—and thus, by definition, making the PCR value different from the expected "known good" value. Thus, malicious software is not able to extend the register back to the known good value.

In addition to extending measurement to a PCR, the platform maintains a log of the objects extended to that PCR. This allows a verifying entity to use the log to validate the PCR content. Another way to look at this is that the log that contains the information and the PCR value validates the log. We will see later that for some applications, it is the final value of the PCR that is of interest and for other applications, it is the log.

Static and Dynamic Measurements

Until now, we have looked at measurements generically, but there are multiple PCRs and thus multiple measurement results. Static measurements are those that are made once each time the platforms boots. There are 16 PCRs reserved for static measurements (PCR0–15). These PCRs are only cleared when the platform powers up or there is a hard reset: that is, a signal to all components (TPM, processors, and chipset) to return them to their power-on state. Static PCRs are used in measuring the platform configuration, as follows:

- PCR0: CRTM, BIOS, and host platform extensions

- PCR1: Host platform configuration

- PCR2: Option ROM code

- PCR3: Option ROM configuration and data

- PCR4: IPL code (usually the MBR)

- PCR5: IPL code configuration and data (for use by the IPL code)

- PCR6: State transition and wake events

- PCR7: Host platform manufacturer control

- PCR8–PCR15: Reserved for the OS; not used by TXT

PCR0 is the primary CRTM PCR and speaks to the integrity of PCR1–PCR7. CRTM stands for Core Root of Trust Measurement (see the "The Intel TXT Boot Sequence" section), which means it is measured first and starts the chain of measurements for the static PCRs. There is also a Dynamic Root of Trust Measurement (DRTM) for the dynamic PCRs.

Dynamic measurements are measurements made to PCRs that can be reset without resetting the platform. There are eight dynamic PCRs, used as follows:

- PCR 16: Reserved for debug; not used by Intel TXT.

- PCR17–PCR20: Reset upon a successful secure launch.

    - PCR17: DRTM and launch control policy

    - PCR18: Trusted OS startup code

    - PCR19: Trusted OS (for example OS configuration)

    - PCR20: Trusted OS (for example OS kernel and other code)

- PCR20–PCR22: Can be reset by the trusted OS while in secure mode. Note that PCR20 is reset at secure launch and by the trusted OS.

    - PCR21: Defined by the trusted OS

    - PCR22: Defined by the trusted OS

- PCR23: Reserved for applications; can be reset and extended by any locality. Outside the scope of Intel TXT.

To summarize, Intel TXT provides the means to securely measure and report various platform components, and thus detect changes in those components. Measured components include:

- Platform Configuration (Static Root of Trust)

    - PCR0: BIOS code

    - PCR1: BIOS settings

    - PCR2: Option ROM code

    - PCR3: Option ROM settings

    - PCR4: Boot Sector - Master Boot Record (MBR)

    - PCR5: Boot configuration

    - PCR6: Platform state changes

- Operating System (Dynamic Root of Trust)

    - Operating system code (PCR18+ OS-specific PCRs)

    - Operating system settings (PCRs are OS-specific)

    - Other components specified by the operating system

These components are divided into two groups because the root-of-trust for those groups is different.

The Intel TXT Boot Sequence

By now, it should be easy to piece together what happens when the platform boots. The boot sequence that generates the static chain of trust measurements goes like this:

1. Processor microcode

    a. Loads BIOS ACM into secure memory internal to the processor to protect it from any outside influence.

    b. Validates that the ACM is authentic using cryptographic signature.

    c. Starts the core root of trust measurement by extending the BIOS ACM measurement to PCR0.

    d. Only if all checks pass, the microcode will

    - Enable ACM mode by enabling access to TPM locality 3 and opening access to TXT private registers.

    - Execute the BIOS ACM startup code.

    - The use of internal secure memory and then validation assures the ACM is free of malicious code before and during execution.

2. BIOS ACM startup code

    a. Measures critical BIOS components.

    b. Extends PCR0 with those measurements.

    c. If the ACM determines that secrets might have been left in memory (i.e., a potential reset attack), it validates that BIOS startup code has not been modified or corrupted. (More about reset attacks to follow.)

    d. Exits ACM mode disabling locality 3 and access to TXT private registers.

    e. Jumps to the BIOS startup code.

3. BIOS

    a. Measures the remainder of the BIOS code and extends PCR0 with those measurements. Does not execute any code until that code has been measured and extended into a PCR.

    b. Configures the platform.

    c. Measures the BIOS configuration and extends that into PCR1.

    d. Calls BIOS ACM using the GETSEC instruction to perform security checks.

    - Processor microcode loads the ACM into secure internal memory and performs the same validation as before. It then enables ACM mode and executes the requested ACM function.

    - ACM performs its security checks, exits ACM mode, and returns to the BIOS.

    e. Finishes platform configuration.

    f.   Calls the BIOS ACM using the GETSEC instruction to lock the BIOS configuration.

- Processor microcode loads ACM into secure internal memory and performs the same validation as before. It then enables ACM mode and executes the requested ACM function.

- ACM performs configuration locking, exits ACM mode, and returns to the BIOS.

  After locking the configuration, the BIOS may execute other firmware.

- Measures any option ROM code (for I/O devices) and extends those measurements into PCR2.

- Executes the option ROM code for each device.

4. Each option ROM

    a.   Measures any hidden option ROM code and extends that measurement into PCR2.

    b.   Configures and enables the device.

    c.   Measures device configuration information and extends that measurement into PCR3.

    d.   Returns to BIOS.

5. BIOS

    a.   Selects a boot device.

    b.   Measures the IPL (Initial Program Load) code, typically the Master Boot Record (MBR), and extends that measurement into PCR4.

    c.   Executes the IPL code.

6. IPL code

    a.   Measures IPL configuration and extends that measurement into PCR5.

    b.   Loads the OS boot loader and executes it.

This sequence is illustrated in Figure 2-4.

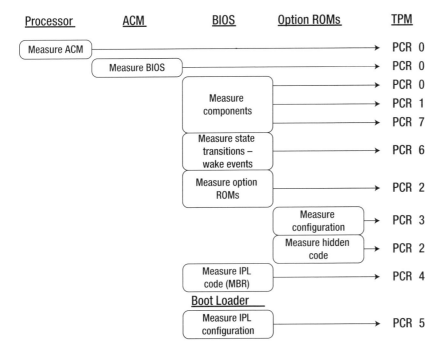

Figure 2-4. *Typical static measurement sequence*

At this point, the BIOS has brought the platform to a state where it is ready to boot the operating system (IPL). Normal bootstrap process is followed where the OS loader gets executed. Typically, what happens for an Intel TXT-enabled OS, instead of loading the first kernel module, the first module loaded is a special Trusted Boot (TBOOT) module. The purpose of the TBOOT module is to initialize the platform for secure mode operation and initiate the Measured Launch Process.

Measured Launch Process (Secure Launch)

This is the part of the technology that controls how and if a host OS can enter the secure mode of execution, and thus becomes a trusted OS. The following are the characteristics of secure mode:

- The trusted OS code has been measured and that measurement is a known good value (as established by the platform owner).

- The trusted OS starts in a deterministic state.

    - All processors except the bootstrap processor are in a special idle state until the OS explicitly starts them up directly in protected mode. This is different from the normal bootstrap process where those processors are started in real mode and have to be transitioned into protected mode. Thus, this removes that window of vulnerability.

    - System Code is protected against access by I/O devices (referred to as Direct Memory Access or DMA).

- The OS has TPM locality 2 access and the dynamic PCRs have been reset to their default values. DRTM PCRs have been extended.

  - PCR17 has been extended with the measurement of the SINIT ACM (that is, the Dynamic Root of Trust Measurement, or DRTM) and the policy that allowed the secure launch.

  - PCR18 has been extended with the measurement of the trusted OS.

What the OS has to do to enter secure mode and start the DRTM is drastically different from what BIOS does for the static root of trust measurements. However, the principles are the same.

Before the host OS enters secure mode, it must put the platform in a known state. The host OS then invokes the GETSEC instruction specifying the SENTER operation. This causes the processor microcode to do the following:

- Load SINIT ACM into secure memory, internal to the processor, in order to protect it from any outside influence.

- Verify that the ACM matches the chipset and that the hash of its public key matches the hash hardcoded into the chipset.

- Validate that the ACM is authentic by verifying its measurement matches its cryptographic signature.

  Again, the use of internal secure memory and then validation assures the ACM is and remains free of malicious code before and during execution.

- Start the dynamic root of trust measurement by clearing PCR17–PCR20 and then extending the SINIT ACM measurement to PCR17.

- Only if all checks pass, the microcode will

  - Enable ACM mode, which enables access to TPM locality 3 and opens access to TXT private registers.

  - Execute the SINIT ACM code.

The SINIT ACM now takes control and does the following:

1. Checks to see if it has been revoked—that is, if a newer version of the SINIT ACM has executed and set the revocation level (stored in the TPM) to indicate this SINIT ACM is an older version that is no longer to be used.

2. Validates that the platform was properly configured by BIOS and that the OS has properly conditioned the platform for a secure launch.

3. Measures the trusted OS code.

4. Executes the Launch Control Policy engine that interprets the launch control policy set by the datacenter to determine if the OS is to be trusted to do a secure launch.

5. If any of these checks fail, it is considered an attack and the ACM issues what is called a *TXT reset*, which prevents a secure launch until the platform has been power-cycled. This assures that no malicious code remains in memory.

6. If these checks pass, then the ACM

   a. Extends PCR17 with the policy it used to allow the launch

   b. Extends PCR18 with the trusted OS measurement

   c. Enables locality 2 access

   d. Exits ACM Mode and jumps to the trusted OS entry point

The trusted OS then takes control and is now able to extend PCR17–PCR22. The trusted OS is in control of what gets extended, and when. For example, the OS could measure additional code into PCR19, trusted OS configuration into PCR20, and extend geographic location into PCR22.

Protection Against Reset Attacks

We briefly discussed how the BIOS had to be trusted to protect against reset attacks. Here is how that protection unfolds.

When the OS successfully performs a secure launch, it sets a special nonvolatile *Secrets* flag to indicate that it has (or will have) secrets and other privileged information in memory. When the trusted OS gracefully shuts down and exits the secure environment, it resets the *Secrets* flag. The flag can only be reset via the trusted OS invoking the GETSEC instruction. This is usually done as part of a graceful shutdown.

If a *reset attack* occurs (that is, a reset before the trusted OS clears the *Secrets* flag), the BIOS ACM (which is the first to execute after the reset) assures that the BIOS scrubs the memory. For desktop and mobile platforms with simpler memory architectures, the BIOS ACM actually clears the memory. However, high-end workstations and servers have more complex memory architectures, so the BIOS must be trusted to scrub the memory. But the ACM does not blindly trust the BIOS, because it could have been corrupted and thus contain malicious code. The ACM uses two methods to verify that the BIOS had not been corrupted: autopromotion and signed BIOS policy. Each OEM selects the method that works best for their platform.

Autopromotion means that the ACM remembers the BIOS measurement and if the platform passed the launch control policy, then that BIOS will be trusted to scrub memory in the event of a reset attack.

Signed BIOS policy allows the OEM to provide a list of known good BIOS measurements signed by the OEM. The signature is validated by a hash measurement of the public key stored in the TPM. Thus, if the BIOS measurement does not match a value in the signed list, or the list signature is not valid, or the list is signed with the wrong key, then BIOS is not considered trusted.

If the ACM is not able to verify that the BIOS is trusted using one of these methods, then it locks the memory controllers. Since this is done before BIOS executes its first instruction, the platforms boots without any memory. We call this a "bricked" system, because a platform without memory is about as useful as a brick. BIOS may be able to recover from a bricked system, if it can restore the BIOS or revert to a BIOS version that will be trusted. Otherwise, the only way to recover is to turn off power and remove the coin battery. This signals the ACM that a person, not malicious software, is in control of the platform.

One point that needs to be mentioned is the potential of a BIOS update to look like a reset attack. First, this is only an issue when the BIOS update is done while the trusted OS is in secure mode (OS present BIOS update) and only if the platform resets before the OS exits the secure environment (that is, doesn't reset the *Secrets* flag). For this case, autopromotion will fail. There are several ways for the OEM to mitigate this problem. One is to use signed BIOS policy. Others are to defer the BIOS image update until the next boot or provide a failsafe BIOS image (*failsafe* means revert to the original BIOS image whose measurement is known to the ACM). There are more, so it is not fair to say signed BIOS policy is better, but platforms incorporating signed BIOS policy can recover from corrupted BIOS without the need to remove the coin battery.

Launch Control Policy

Intel TXT includes a policy engine that permits the datacenter to specify what is a known good platform configuration and which system software is permitted to do a secure launch. The term for this feature is *launch control policy* (LCP). In Chapter 4, we will go into detail on how to create a launch control policy and provide guidance on selecting a policy. For now, let's focus on the mechanics.

There are actually two policy engines: one in the BIOS ACM that controls the policy used to validate the BIOS integrity when there is a reset attack and one in the SINIT ACM that enforces the launch control policy. We have already discussed the BIOS policy engine in the "Protection Against Reset Attacks" section.

There are two authorities for launch control policy: the *platform supplier* (the OEM) and the *platform owner* (the datacenter). The platform supplier policy is sometimes referred to as the *default policy* because it is created by the OEM before the platform ships. Typically, the platform supplier's default policy will allow any host OS to perform a secure launch on any platform configuration. That is not very exciting, so let's talk about the platform owner policy, what it does, and how it overrides the default policy.

There are two elements to a launch control policy:

- The specification of valid platform configurations (called the PCONF element).

- The specification of OS versions that are allowed to perform a secure launch
  (called the Measured Launch Environment, or MLE element).

The LCP engine analyzes these two elements independently of each other, but both must be satisfied. That is, any OS in the MLE element may perform a secure launch on any platform by the PCONF element. In addition, the result of omitting the PCONF element is that all platform configurations are allowed. Likewise, the result of omitting the MLE element means that any system software is allowed to perform a secure launch on a platform with a valid platform configuration.

Platform Configuration (PCONF)

So how does one specify the platform configuration? Since BIOS went through all the trouble to measure everything into PCRs, the PCONF policy element uses those measurements. Only the first seven PCRs convey platform configuration information.

- PCR0: BIOS code

- PCR1: BIOS settings

- PCR2: Option ROM code

- PCR3: Option ROM settings

- PCR4: Boot sector - Master Boot Record (MBR)

- PCR5: Boot configuration

- PCR6: Platform state changes

The policy authority (for example, the datacenter manager) selects which PCRs are relevant and creates a composite hash from those PCR values. The Intel TXT architecture actually allows selection of any of the PCRs. The data structure that specifies which PCRs were selected and the composite hash is called a *PCRInfo*. The PCONF element can hold any number of PCRInfo structures (the actual limit is greater than 100 million). Typically, only a few PCRInfos are needed per platform.

For each PCRInfo, the policy engine will create a composite hash from the actual values of the specified PCRs and compare that to the composite hash in the policy. If they match, it means all of the selected PCRs have the correct value, and thus the platform configuration is trusted. If none of the PCRInfos produce a match, then the platform is not trusted and there can be no secure launch.

Trusted OS Measurements (MLE Element)

By now you are probably thinking that the MLE does the same thing but with the dynamic PCRs (PCR17–PCR22); however, that's not correct. PCR0–PCR7 values are stable after IPL, but dynamic PCRs are at their default values. Thus, the MLE element simply contains a list of known good TBOOT measurements that are compared to the TBOOT hash value measured by the ACM. That hash value will only be extended into PCR18 if LCP passes. In other words, the policy engine will calculate the hash of the trusted OS and compare that measurement to the list of measurements in the MLE element. If it matches any one of them, then the OS is trusted to perform a secure launch.

Protecting Policies

So how are the policies protected against tampering? The answer is: using the TPM NVRAM. But a policy can consume a large number of bytes—more than the TPM NVRAM provides. Thus, the policy is split in part into TPM policy data stored in the TPM NVRAM (referred to as *NV policy data*) and in an optional *policy data structure* (stored in a file) that holds the PCONF and MLE elements (that is, it contains the lists of allowed platform and MLE measurements). The policy data structure is optional, because a policy that allows any platform configuration and any OS does not need PCONF and MLE elements.

The platform owner creates a specific TPM NVRAM index (40000001) called the *PO policy* index with a property that only allows the platform owner to write that data (which is the small NV policy data mentioned earlier). One of the fields of the NV policy data is a hash value, which is the hash measurement of the optional policy data structure.

The policy engine calculates the hash of the policy data structure and compares it to the hash value stored in the TPM. If the policy data structure had been compromised, the hash values won't compare, and thus the policy will fail.

Sealing

Earlier, it was stated that measurements are used for many purposes. One of those purposes is the sealing of secrets. Data can be sealed to one or more PCR values. Sealing is the act of having the TPM encrypt a block of data so that it cannot be decrypted unless the specified PCRs have the correct values. The caller specifies the PCRs and their composite hash when it passes the TPM the block of data. The TPM returns an encrypted "blob."

Later, the software can ask the TPM to decrypt the blob. The TPM will only decrypt it if the current PCR values match what was specified at the time the data was sealed.

Let's look an example to see how sealing could work to protect sensitive data. Upon installing an OS, that OS creates a symmetric encryption key, which it uses to encrypt data that it stores on disk. The OS seals that key, specifying its own PCR18 value, and then saves the blob to disk. Each time the OS boots up, it has the TPM unseal the blob, which provides the OS with the key it uses to encrypt and decrypt data going to and from disk. Because the data was sealed to PCR18, only that OS is able to unseal the blob—and thus only that OS is able to decrypt the data.

Any other system software will have a different PCR18 measurement, and thus could not unseal the blob. Even if an attacker is able to reverse assemble the OS code, it is not able to gain knowledge of the disk encryption key. Since each platform has a unique disk encryption key, knowledge of a key used on one platform is of no value on other platforms.

Attestation

We have seen how the PCR measurements can be used to set launch control policy, determine who can access TPM NVRAM, and used to seal data. Now let's discuss the value of those measurements to applications both internal and external to the platform.

Because of the uniqueness property of cryptographic hashes, PCR values and their logs can be used to identify exactly what version of software is executing, as well as its environment.

Several key concepts come into play:

- The TPM protects the measurements.

- The combination of TXT hardware and ACMs guarantee the accuracy of the static root of trust measurement and the dynamic root of trust measurement.

- The combination of authentic root of trust measurement and chain of trust principle (requiring any code that is able to extend a PCR to be measured prior to its execution) enforces the ability to detect tampering.

- The TPM provides a "TPM Quote" where the TPM signs the PCR values to assure that values are not maliciously or inadvertently modified in transit. This guarantees authenticity of the measurements.

This accuracy, security, and dependability mean applications can use these measurements to make their own trust decisions. Unfortunately, other properties of the cryptographic hash make it difficult to use the values directly. This is where an attestation authority comes into play. An *attestation authority* (similar to a certification authority) is a trusted third-party entity that is able to authenticate the PCR values and translate those values by comparing them with a database of known good values.

There are several models for attestation. One is where the application retrieves the PCR values and uses an attestation service to authenticate that the target platform is, in fact, what it claims to be. Another model is where the attestation authority retrieves the PCRs from the target platform and provides the translated results to its client applications.

Either way, the client application is able to determine or confirm (among other things) the type of platform, the OS vendor, and exact version of system software that is executing on the target platform.

Another method (known as *whitelisting*) is where the attestation authority maintains a list of known good results and simply validates if the target platform meets one of the trusted profiles.

Later, we will discuss how this information is used to enforce policies set by cloud service clients.

Summary

Intel Trusted Execution Technology is compliant with the TCG PC Client and Servers Specifications. Cryptographic secure hashing algorithms generate unique measurements of platform components, platform configuration, system software, and software configuration. Those measurements are stored in PCRs protected by the TPM. Each PCR may contain multiple measurements and the PCR log identifies each element that was measured to that PCR. The value in the PCR can be used to verify the log.

PCR0 contains the static root of trust measurement, as well as BIOS code measurements. These measurements cannot be spoofed because they are rooted in hardware. The validity of PCR1–PCR7 rests on the validity of PCR0. That is, PCR1–PCR7 can only be trusted if the PCR0 measurement is known to be good.

PCR17 contains the dynamic root of trust measurement, as well as policy measurements. These measurements cannot be spoofed because they are rooted in hardware. PCR18 contains the measurement of the trusted OS. The validity of PCR18 rests on the validity of PCR17. PCR19–PCR22 usage is OS-specific—their purpose is defined by the trusted OS. Therefore, their values can only be trusted and interpreted if PCR18 is a known good value.

The platform owner controls what is considered a valid platform configuration, and thus which OS is allowed to perform a secure launch. An OS in secure mode has demonstrated compliance with the datacenter's launch control policy, and thus has TPM locality 2 access. The secure launch (more accurately referred to as a *measured launch*) means that the OS's measurements have been extended into the dynamic PCRs, and therefore the OS is able to seal data to its own unique measurement.

PCRs and their logs can attest to the type, health, and state of a platform to both local and remote applications. Those applications are able to use that information to make their own policy decisions.

■ ■ ■

CHAPTER 3

Getting It to Work: Provisioning Intel® TXT

Now that we have an understanding of what it means for a platform to implement Intel® Trusted Execution Technology, the next step is to put that technology into operation. This chapter describes the general steps that a platform owner (typically an IT organization) must take to enable Intel® TXT, and then identifies the steps to condition the platform to realize its values.

■ **Note**   Intel provides a list of platforms that have demonstrated compliance with Intel Trusted Execution Technology. This list can be found at `www.intel.com/content/www/us/en/architecture-and-technology/trusted-execution-technology/trusted-execution-technology-server-platforms-matrix.html`, or just go to `Intel.com` and search for Intel Trusted Execution Technology.

Provisioning a New Platform

Unfortunately, the default configuration for new platforms requires the owner to "opt in" to using Intel Trusted Execution Technology. Thus, the owner must explicitly enable Intel TXT, which includes a series of steps that must be performed to take advantage of the technology. These steps are necessary to protect owners that are not yet ready to take advantage of Intel TXT, such as protection from malicious software that could otherwise hijack the TPM and Intel TXT resources. The steps to provision the platform are as follows:

1. Enable and activate the TPM.
2. Enable supporting technology.
3. Enable Intel TXT.
4. Provision the TPM.
    a. Establish TPM ownership.
    b. Create a platform owner policy index.
5. Create a platform owner launch control policy.
6. Install a trusted operating system.

BIOS Setup

The first steps are accomplished via the BIOS Setup menu. We wish we could provide explicit instructions, but each platform manufacturer has their own style for BIOS menus, so the actual steps that need to be performed will vary from manufacturer to manufacturer, and possibly even between platform types. But let's walk through the process.

Enable and Activate the Trusted Platform Module (TPM)

This step is typically accomplished via the *Security* tab of the BIOS setup menu. Most BIOS implementations require setting the BIOS's *administrator password* before the BIOS will perform TPM operations. In some cases, the menu might allow you to select the "TPM enable" operation, but it does not perform that operation if the password has not been set. So it is best to set BIOS passwords before attempting any TPM operations. Besides, it is always good practice to set the BIOS password to help protect against unauthorized changes.

Unfortunately, the BIOS will not honor TPM commands at the same time that the password is set. So the actual steps will be to set the password, save and exit, and then reenter the BIOS setup to enable the TPM.

The BIOS menu might show *TPM status*. TPM status could take any of the four combinations of *Enabled/Disabled* and *Activated/Deactivated*. Most BIOS menus provide a "TPM command" that allows selection of the following:

- No operation
- Clear (or Clear Ownership)
- Enable/Turn On/Activate TPM
- Disable/Turn Off /Inactivate TPM

The terms will vary, but the effect is the same. For example, on a Dell PowerEdge R410, you will find this control on the *Security* tab listed as *TPM Status … Disabled/Deactivated*. You will need to select *Enable/Activate TPM*. For this example, you also need to set *TPM Security* to *On with Pre-boot Measurements*. Next select *save and exit*, which causes the platform to reset. The platform has to reset for the TPM state to change—this is a security feature of the TPM. If the BIOS does have separate *Enable* and *Activate* controls, then you will need to perform the following steps: Enable TPM, save and exit, Activate TPM, save and exit.

All of these platform resets can be time consuming, but if they are skipped, it is possible that the action is ignored. If performed properly, the TPM status should indicate that the TPM is enabled and activated. There is an effort underway to streamline/automate enabling the TPM, referred to as the *physical presence interface* that allows system software to request these operations and have the BIOS prompt the operator to "accept or reject."

Enable Supporting Technology

Intel TXT requires that Intel® Virtualization Technology (Intel® VT) is enabled. The steps to enabling Intel VT also vary by platform manufacturer. Some platforms might have a single control under the *Processor* tab to enable virtualization technology (this is the case with the Dell PowerEdge 410), or the platform might provide a control to enable VMX (virtualization instructions) under the *Processor* tab and another control to enable Intel Virtualization Technology for Directed I/O (Intel VT-d) on a separate chipset or I/O tab. In this case, both controls must be enabled. Various virtualization options (such as enabling SR-IOV) can be set as desired.

Intel TXT requires that VMX is enabled so that the system software can use it for isolation and protection of software processes (preventing them from accessing private, sensitive, or protected data) and that Intel VT-d is enabled so that the system software can use it to prevent hardware devices from accessing private, sensitive, or protected data.

Enabling Intel® TXT

In many cases, this step must be done after enabling the TPM and enabling Intel Virtualization Technology. Otherwise, the option to enable Intel TXT might be hidden or disabled.

In most cases, this control is found on the *Processor* tab or on the *Security* tab. Not everyone titles that control "Intel TXT" or has the same requirement. Regardless of what it is called, set it to enable *Intel TXT measured boot*, and then save and exit.

For our example, on a Dell PowerEdge R410, you will find this control on the *Security* tab listed as *Intel TXT* (see Figure 3-1). However, before you can enable it, you need to set *TPM Security* to *On with Pre-boot Measurements*. You can find the requirements by highlighting the *Intel TXT* control and pressing F1.

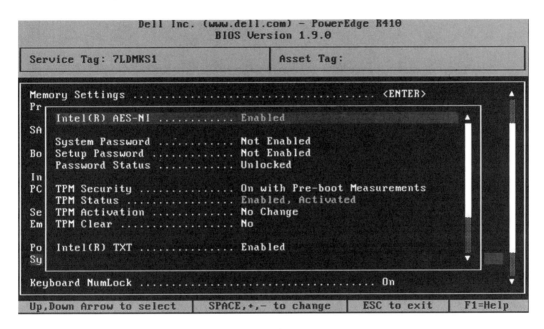

Figure 3-1. *BIOS security screen*

Summary of BIOS Setup

The following summarizes the BIOS setup:

1. Set the BIOS password.

2. Save and exit.

3. Enable/activate TPM.

4. Save and exit.

5. Enable virtualization (VMX and Intel VT-d).

6. May need to save and exit.

7. Enable Intel TXT.

8. Save and exit.

Automating BIOS Provisioning

As mentioned earlier, there is an effort underway to automate enabling of the TPM, called the *physical presence interface*. Intel is publishing an extension to that capability that allows system software to also request the enabling of Intel Virtualization Technology and Intel Trusted Execution Technology at the same time. With the physical presence interface, the operator would see a single prompt to accept or reject the request to enable everything needed to enable Intel TXT. I bring this up because the manual steps to enable Intel TXT are a real pain, not to mention very time consuming (multiple resets, and because more powerful servers take longer to boot, more time). But as the technology matures, it will become more user-friendly. It's all part of the *crawl-walk-run* paradigm.

The other good news is that there is at least one third-party company producing "*How To*" automation guides for a number of the more popular platforms, and another is working on providing automated provisioning scripts as part of its platform management suite.

Establish TPM Ownership

This step has significant dependencies on the particular host OS/VMM that is to be installed. In some cases, the OS/VMM installation must perform this step. Having the OS/VMM installation automatically perform this step definitely makes it easier, but does restrict the platform to a single host operating system. In the past, this might have been a problem because it could prevent repurposing[1] of the platform. However, virtualization technology (virtual machines) provides a better solution for managing time-varying workloads, so this should not be an issue.

What Is TPM Ownership? Why Is This Important?

TPM ownership means that an authority (the OS or the datacenter) has set a password that must be used to allocate TPM resources. An entity that knows that password is considered the TPM owner and is able to specify access rights for TPM resources. In addition, certain TPM commands can only be issued by the TPM owner.

When a new platform arrives, the TPM is in an unowned state. Before any TPM objects and resources can be allocated, a TPM owner must be established. This is accomplished via a *Take Ownership* command issued to the TPM, which provides the TPM with a secret value that is only known by the TPM and the TPM owner. In essence, this is a password. It is a strong password or, more likely, the hash of a password/phrase (since the "secret" is 20 bytes—the size of a SHA-1 hash digest). Once ownership has been established, the TPM's *Take Ownership* operation is no longer available.

Thus, the first entity that successfully performs the *Take Ownership* operation becomes the TPM owner. This is one of the reasons that the TPM is initially in a disabled/inactive state—to prevent malicious software from taking ownership. Thus, you should only enable the TPM immediately before you are ready to establish ownership.

Anyone that knows the secret value (or can generate it by hashing the password/passphrase) is considered the TPM owner, and thus can perform owner authorized operations on the TPM. The role of the TPM owner will become more apparent as we discuss tools to set launch control policy, allocate TPM NVRAM, create keys, and so on.

How to Establish TPM Ownership

Some OS/VMMs require that they perform the take ownership operation (typically during the installation process or the first boot) and others expect the datacenter to establish ownership. Why is this? Well, the TPM and Intel TXT were architected with flexibility in mind. Thus, various OSV/VMM vendors make use of the TPM in different ways. To better understand why, let's look at three TPM management models. The following models are all valid and illustrate various considerations for establishing TPM ownership and managing the TPM.

---

[1]Repurposing of a system is where the platform reboots for a different purpose. One example is where a server used during normal working hours as a file server would be repurposed at night to serve as a backup server.

Pass-Through TPM Model

Figure 3-2 illustrates a simple management model in which a TPM management utility resides as an application on the server. The host OS/VMM simply provides TPM access to the application, and the management utility establishes a session with the TPM. In this scenario (for performing owner authorized operations), the utility prompts the user for the TPM password and uses it to establish the session with the TPM. It is this same TPM utility that initially establishes TPM ownership and later performs TPM operations that require owner authorization (such as setting owner policy). Many Linux operating systems support this model.

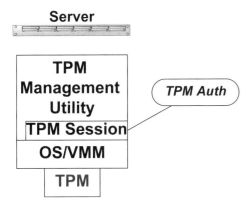

Figure 3-2. *Local TPM management*

The TPM management application can be supplied by the OS/VMM vendor or by a third party. If the OS/VMM or other entity needs to perform authorized actions, then they will need to prompt the user for the TPM password.

Remote Pass-Through TPM Model

Figure 3-3 illustrates an adaptation of the locally managed model where the TPM management utility is executed on a remote management console. Because the TPM command/response is communicated across a network, the management utility would create a secure transport session with the TPM if it needs to protect the data in the command/response while in flight. Other than the use of a secure channel, this model functions the same as the local management model.

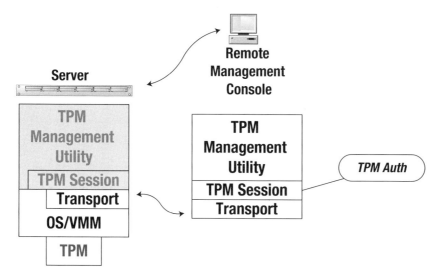

Figure 3-3. *Remote TPM management*

This model does not preclude executing the TPM management utility locally, and any operating system that supports local pass-through should also be able to support this model.

Management Server Model

Figure 3-4 illustrates a model where TPM management is integrated with other server management utilities in a central management server. Unlike the previous models, the management server would be the TPM owner—that is, perform *TPM Take Ownership* and therefore track the TPM authorization value for each of the compute servers. This model supports each TPM having a unique TPM owner authorization value or all servers in the managed pool might have the same owner authorization value. Either way, (other than the TPMs themselves) only the central management server knows the authorization values. VMware ESXi supports this style of TPM management.

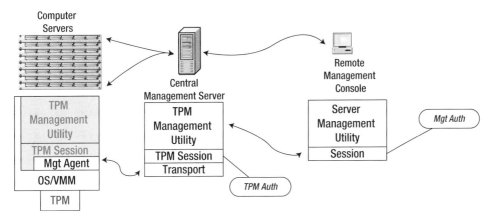

Figure 3-4. *Central management server*

A central management server is able to enforce more granular control over which TPM operations are authorized by a particular client.

For example, the datacenter manager might have complete access to all TPM commands, whereas other management support personnel are limited to a subset that fits their particular jobs. Clients that use the management service to manage their applications have little or no TPM management capability.

One main benefit of the central management server is that each client of the management server only needs to know his or her own password to log into the management server and does not have to track TPM passwords.

Protecting Authorization Values

It should be noted that the TPM secret authorization value is never transmitted as part of the command data. Rather, the initiator of a command that requires authentication proves it knows the authentication value by computing the hash of the TPM command data, plus a nonce provided by the TPM, plus the TPM authorization value. The initiator sends that hash result with the TPM command, as illustrated in Figure 3-5. As we learned in the previous chapter, this is the Hash Method of Authentication (HMAC). The TPM authenticates that the initiator knows the correct authorization value by performing a hash of the command data, expected nonce, and the TPM's copy of the Owner Authorization value; this result must match the hash sent with the command or else the TPM rejects the command. Thus it is not possible to derive the TPM authorization value by monitoring the communication.

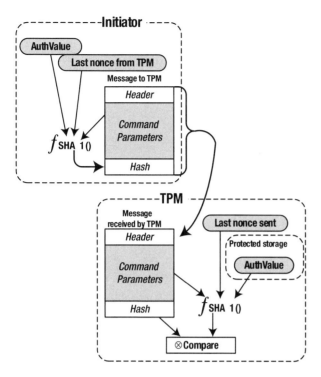

Figure 3-5. *TPM command authentication process*

The nonce prevents replay attacks because the nonce randomizes the HMAC hash value. Each response from the TPM provides a new nonce that the initiator must use in the next command. Thus the exact same command has a different expected HMAC value each time it is sent. The TPM response is also protected by the use of a different nonce (one that the initiator includes in the command data), which the TPM then uses to generate the response HMAC value. In summary, the HMAC in the command proves to the TPM that the initiator is authorized and that the message had not been altered. The HMAC in the response proves to the initiator that the response came from the TPM and had not been altered.

Perhaps you were wondering how the *Take Ownership* command works without sending the owner authorization value in the clear since the TPM does not yet know the TPM secret password. To protect the secret value from being snooped, the TPM provides the initiator with the public portion of an asymmetric *endorsement key* and the prospective TPM owner uses it to encrypt the secret value when it sends the *Take Ownership* command. The endorsement key is a unique RSA encryption key pair created by the TPM vendor for the TPM at the time the TPM was manufactured. The user can read the public encryption key, but only the TPM knows the private decryption key. Thus only the TPM can decrypt the encrypted value. The TPM then uses that decrypted value to authenticate the *Take Ownership* command and all subsequent commands that require owner authorization.

A couple of points of interest: the TPM owner can gracefully change the owner authorization value using a TPM *Change Owner Auth* command. Additionally, in case the owner disposes of the platform or forgets the TPM owner authorization value, the BIOS does have the means to clear the TPM's owner authorization value (and storage root key) so that the *Take Ownership* process is again enabled. However, this action destroys all objects (such as TPM NVRAM indexes) that require owner authorization. Likewise, any keys or external entities that were sealed to the TPM are rendered useless. So the *BIOS Clear Ownership* action essentially returns the TPM to its initial state and cannot be used to recover a lost TPM password. Thus, if you lose the TPM password, the only resolution is to clear ownership and start from scratch. The TPM owner also has a command that is equivalent to the *BIOS Clear Ownership*, except it does not require resetting the platform and entering the BIOS setup menu. Either one is an excellent way for a datacenter manager to revoke all keys and objects protected by the TPM before selling, transferring, or otherwise disposing of a server platform.

Install a Trusted Host Operating System

There is no change in how the OS/VMM is installed, but you will need to know the TPM ownership requirement of the particular OS/VMM being installed. Many OS/VMMs support "zero-touch" automatic or scripted installs, including Intel TXT settings.

Depending on the OS/VMM, you might have to modify the startup code to instruct the OS to perform a measured launch (see the following "Linux Example"). This assures that the first OS code loaded is the Trusted Boot (called TBOOT) code that sets up the platform for Intel TXT and initiates the measured launch before loading the OS kernel. This was true for most Linux operating systems when I started writing this book, but I have been informed that many of the major Linux OSVs are now making it simple by providing the modified grub files. So check with your favorite OSV for the requirements to enable Intel TXT.

VMware ESXi Example

VMware ESXi requires that the TPM be in an unowned state or (for the case of reinstalling) ownership previously established by a VMware central management server). The install program automatically installs its Intel TXT components. It is the runtime operation that checks if the TPM is present and if the platform supports Intel TXT.

Each time a VMware ESXi server boots, it checks if the TPM is enabled but not owned. If so, it performs the take ownership operation to establish itself as the TPM owner. After that, it checks if Intel TXT is enabled, and if it is, the VMM performs a measured launch and enters secure mode. Note that this allows you to install ESXi before enabling the TPM and/or enabling Intel TXT—but I still recommend that you follow the prescribed order.

Thus a new server is ready for loading ESXi after performing the BIOS setup steps (see "BIOS Setup" at the beginning of this chapter). If you are reprovisioning a server (that is, installing ESXi after installing a different OS/VMM), then you need to execute the Clear TPM Ownership action from the BIOS menu and re-enable the TPM before installing ESXi.

Linux Example (Ubuntu)

After installing the OS, follow these steps to enable the Intel TXT–measured launch. As noted earlier, these steps might no longer be required, depending on the OS version.

1. Install TBOOT.

   a. Install modules.

      ```
      $ apt-get install tboot
      ```

   b. Change to the /boot directory.

   c. Verify that tboot.gz is there.

2. Copy SINIT ACM to the /boot directory.

   – For 5600 series platforms, you will need to download SINIT ACM (X5600_SINIT_16. BIN) from http://software.intel.com/en-us/articles/intel-trusted-execution-technology/ (scroll down to "Server Platforms").

   – For newer platforms, the BIOS image contains the SINIT ACM; however, you may download the latest SINIT ACM from that same web site and the OS will use the most recent.

3. Install and verify the TCG software stack.

    a. Install.

    ```
    $ apt-get install trousers
    $ apt-get install trousers-dbg
    $ apt-get update
    ```

    b. Verify them by running TCSD daemon.

    ```
    $ tcsd
    ```

4. Edit the GRUB menu. It is best to copy a menu item and then alter it. To modify the
   following grub menu item:

   ```
   title    Ubuntu 11.10, kernel 3.0.0-12-server
   kernel   /boot/vmlinuz-3.0.0-12-server root=/dev/sda1 ro quiet splash
   initrd   /boot/initrd.img-3.0.0-server
   quiet
   ```

   a. Modify the *title* to indicate Trusted Boot.

   b. Change *kernel* and *initrd* lines to be modules.

   c. Add "kernel   /boot/tboot.gz logging=memory" before those module definitions.

   d. Add the SINIT module for the platform after those module definitions; for example:

   ```
   Module   /boot/X5600_SINIT_16.BIN
   ```

   e. The modified grub menu item should look like this:

   ```
   title    Trusted Boot - Ubuntu 11.10, kernel 3.0.0-12-server
   kernel   /boot/tboot.gz logging=memory
   module   /boot/vmlinuz-3.0.0-12-server root=/dev/sda1 ro quiet splash
   module   /boot/initrd.img-3.0.0-server
   module   /boot/X5600_SINIT_16.BIN
   ```

5. Verify that the platform performs the measured launch.

   a. Reboot the server.

   ```
   $ reboot
   ```

   b. Select the new menu item from the grub menu.

   c. Run TXT-stat; it should show TXT Measured Launch = TRUE.

   ```
   $ tcsd
   $ txt-stat
   ```

   d. Query the device file to read the PCRs (PCRs 17, 18, and 19 will be populated. If not,
      those PCRs' values will contain the default value of FF FF FF ... FF).

   ```
   $ cat /sys/class/misc/tpm0/device/pcrs
   ```

If these steps were successful, the platfrom performed the measured launch and PCRs 17–19 contain the SINIT
and OS measurements.

Create Platform Owner's Launch Control Policy

The launch control policy (LCP) is the first owner-controlled use of attestation. That is, the first chance that the owner has to make a trust decision based on attestation measurements made by Intel TXT. The launch control policy allows the platform owner to control which platform configurations and which operating systems are considered trusted.

The next chapter provides a guide to help you in choosing a launch control policy that best suits the datacenter. In this chapter, we concentrate on what launch control policy does, why it is important, and what impact it has.

Before we get down to the details, let me inject some insight. There are some subjective questions that one must answer and your opinion outweighs mine. Those questions are

- Is remote attestation needed if there is a strong launch control policy?

- Is a launch control policy needed if there is a remote attestation?

- Are appropriate tools available to create and manage the policies?

The simplest policy is "ANY" because it defers the policy decision to a later time and allows any platform configuration and any OS. I predict that in the early stages, datacenter managers will find it prudent to select a launch control policy of ANY because it is less complicated and the tools for managing a more complex policy are either not available or not very intuitive. In addition, managing a complex policy can be problematic. I expect this to change as the technology matures and datacenters have better tools and more experience. The more paranoid you are, the faster you will want to transition to a stronger policy. We will discuss these topics in the next chapter, but for now, let's take an objective look at launch control policy.

How It Works

Let's take a closer look at the measured launch process illustrated in Figure 3-6. In particular, the TBOOT module will setup the platform for a measured launch and then invoke the SENTER command.

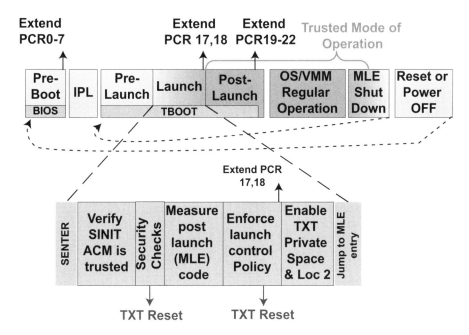

Figure 3-6. *Measured launch timeline*

For the OS/VMM to do a measured launch, it places its trusted post-launch code (referred to as *measured launch environment*, or MLE code) in contiguous memory, fills in a table that indicates where the code resides, and where the platform owner's LCP data structure resides. It then invokes the GetSec SENTER processor instruction.

The processor microcode loads the SINIT ACM (the authenticated code module provided by and signed by Intel) into special protected memory inside the processor, where it validates the ACM and then executes it. Part of the ACM contains the Launch Control Policy Engine that processes the launch control policy.

A launch control policy actually consists of two physical parts, as illustrated in Figure 3-7. Those parts are as follows:

- *NV Policy Data*: A small piece stored in a well-known TPM NVRAM location that uses TPM protections to prevent unauthorized alteration.

- *Policy Data Structure*: Contains a variable amount of policy information (lists of known good measurements). The policy data structure is protected from unauthorized alteration by storing the hash measurement of that structure in the TPM NV policy data.

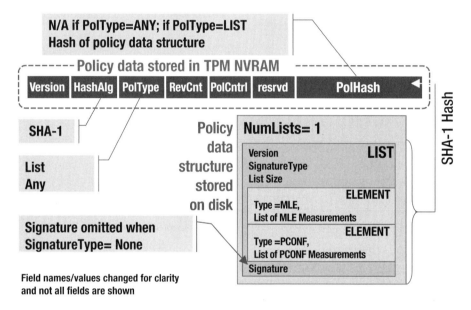

Figure 3-7. *Launch control policy*

The ACM validates the integrity of the policy data structure by measuring it and comparing its measurement to the one stored in the NV policy data. Any attempt by malicious software to modify or replace the platform owner's policy will be detected by the ACM, which results in a *TXT reset*. A TXT reset means that the platform has detected a threat and disables further attempts to perform a measured launch (at least until the platform is power-cycled). Only if the policy data structure is valid will the ACM continue to process the launch control policy.

What LCP Does

Essentially, the LCP is a go/no go decision that determines if the OS/VMM is permitted to do a measured launch (as illustrated in Figure 3-8). This policy is evaluated at the time the OS/VMM initiates a measured launch. There are several parts to the policy decision:

- Specifying which platform configurations are trusted (PCONF policy)
- Specifying which OS/VMMs are trusted (MLE policy)
- Specifying what ACM versions are trusted (SINIT policy)
- Overriding the platform's default policy set by the platform supplier

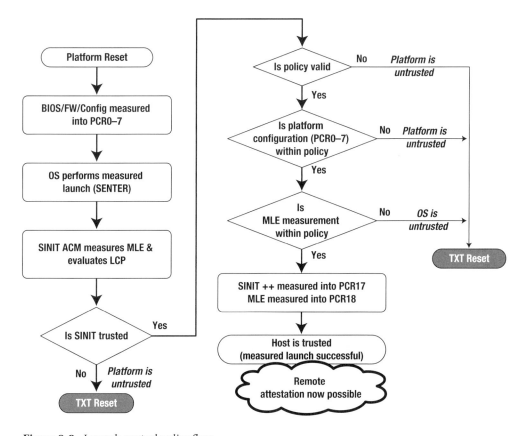

Figure 3-8. *Launch control policy flow*

A tool for creating the policy is illustrated in Figure 3-9. The user has the option to set the SINIT policy by specifying the minimum SINIT version. Under the CONTROL options, the user can also select whether to include SINIT capabilities in the PCR17 measurement. This will impact the PCR17 value for remote attestation, but has no impact on passing the launch control policy. The user selects a *policy type* of ANY or LIST. Selecting LIST displays the LIST information. Since a policy may contain up to eight lists, the tool allows the user to create a list or select an existing list to view, modify, or delete. Selecting LIST also means that the tool will create a policy data structure, calculate the hash measurement of the policy data structure, and use that list hash when it generates the NV policy data. Currently, the only hash algorithm supported is SHA1. We can expect additional algorithm choices in the future to support countries like China that require a different hash algorithm.

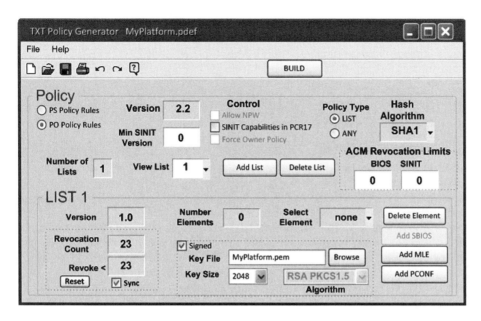

***Figure 3-9.** Policy generator*

Each list may be signed or unsigned. Signed lists allow the manager to update the policy data structure without changing the NV policy data (because the hash measurement of a signed list only covers the public key used to verify that the list is authentic). This makes it easier to update policy by pushing new policy "down the wire" or use a file server for policy administration. Any update to an unsigned list requires the NV policy data to be updated with the new hash measurement of the policy data structure. And of course this requires a TPM NVRAM operation. In our opinion, signing a list is much simpler than updating TPM NVRAM—especially considering that you would need to perform the TPM update on every platform to which the policy change applies.

A signed list has a *revocation count* that is incremented each time the list is modified. The user may select *Sync* to synchronize the *Revoke* value with the *Revocation Count* value or manually set it. The *Revoke* value is part of the NV policy data and means that the corresponding list with a *Revocation* count less than the *Revoke* value will not be allowed. Since the *Revoke* value is held in the NV policy data, it is not applied until the manager updates the TPM NV policy data. Updating the *Revoke* value in the NV policy data typically is not necessary unless the manager is removing a PCONF or MLE measurement and wants to prevent that configuration or OS/VMM from performing a measured launch.

I should probably explain this better. Take for example that you have a signed list allowing OS versions 1.1, 1.2, and 2.1. Let's assume its *Revocation Count* is 2 and the *Revoke* value in the NV policy data is 0. You then update the policy data structure (PDS) with a new signed list that only allows versions 2.1 and 2.2 because 1.x has a security flaw. The revocation counter is automatically incremented to 3 in the list; however, the *Revoke* value in the NV policy data does not change. A potential attack would be for an attacker to replace the new *PDS* with a copy of the old PDS and then cause the platform to boot an older version of the OS so it can exploit the vulnerability. The way to prevent this is to update the *Revoke* value in the NV policy data. When you update the *Revoke* value in the NV policy data to be the same as the new list (3), then the SINIT LCP engine will reject the older signed list (because its *Revocation Count* is less than the allowed value). The *Revocation Count* is protected by the signature, so it cannot be maliciously altered. If you feel confident that the older versions don't pose a threat (either they don't have a vulnerability or there are other protections that prevent OS rollback), then there is no need to update the TPM NVRAM when generating a new signed list.

OK, so let's get back to discussing what is in a policy list. Each list may contain zero or one PCONF element and zero or one MLE element. Note that an SBIOS element is only valid in a platform supplier policy and is not used for the launch control policy.

Specifying Platform Configuration: The PCONF Element

The launch control policy allows the platform owner to specify what is considered an acceptable platform configuration. In the policy generator, the manager would select *Add PCONF* and the tool would display PCONF information, as illustrated in Figure 3-10.

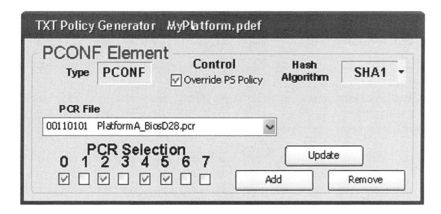

Figure 3-10. *PCONF policy generator*

Up to this point, we have revealed that a set of measurements has been made and stored in protected *Platform Configuration Registers* (PCRs). This starts with the "static root of trust" measurement, which is stored in PCR 0 and the platform firmware makes additional measurements into PCRs 0–7.

- PCR0 - CRTM, BIOS, and Host Platform Extensions

- PCR1 - Host Platform Configuration

- PCR2 - Option ROM Code

- PCR3 - Option ROM Configuration and Data

- PCR4 - IPL Code (usually the MBR)

- PCR5 - IPL Code Configuration and Data (for use by the IPL Code)

- PCR6 - State Transition and Wake Events

- PCR7 - Host Platform Manufacturer Control

These first eight PCRs can be thought of as measuring the platform configuration. However, you might not want to include all of these in the matrix that determines if the platform configuration is trusted. For example, if you were concerned only in assuring the BIOS has not been corrupted and that the Master Boot Record has not been altered, then you would only need to specify that PCR0 and PCR4 contain expected values.

Intel TXT allows the platform owner to specify a set of *PCRInfo structures*, where each PCRInfo structure describes an acceptable platform configuration and the content of a PCRInfo specifies which PCRs are to be considered (and the resulting hash of those PCRs). We refer to this set of PCRInfos as the platform configuration (PCONF) policy.

The policy generator allows the manager to add a new PCRInfo to the PCONF policy or select an existing one to delete or modify. To be able to create a PCRInfo, the tool needs the PCR values. The PCR Dump tool performs this task and is run on the platform that is being added to the policy. The PCR Dump tool captures all of the PCR measurements so that the manager can specify any combination of PCRs. The manager simply selects the PCR dump file and specifies which PCRs. In Figure 3-10, we see that the user selected PCRs 0, 2, 4, and 5 from a PCR dump file named PlatformA_BiosD28.pcr. When the user builds the policy, the generator will create a PCRInfo by generating a hash of the PCR0, 2, 4, and 5 values from the specified PCR file. The user specifies as many PCRInfos as desired, each specifying a PCR file name and set of PCRs. However, what is placed in the policy data structure is only the list of PCRInfo (that is, the PCR selections and respective composite hashes.

At the time of the measured launch, the policy engine evaluates each PCRInfo in the PCONF policy until it finds a match. It evaluates a PCRInfo by reading the current values of the specified PCRs, creating a composite hash from them, and comparing that result to the composite hash specified in the PCRInfo. A match means that the specified PCRs contain the exact same measurement values that were used in calculating the PCRInfo. Thus, the platform has a known acceptable configuration.

If there is no PCONF policy element (this is not the same as no PCRInfos) then the PCONF policy equates TRUE. If one of the PCRInfos evaluates TRUE, then the PCONF policy evaluates TRUE. Otherwise (no PCRInfos match), the PCONF policy evaluates FALSE, which means the platform configuration is not in policy, which results in a *TXT reset*.

One last point, there may be multiple lists in the policy data structure and each list may contain a PCONF element. For the PCONF policy to pass, it only requires a match in any of the elements.

Specifying Trusted Operating Systems: The MLE Element

The launch control policy allows the platform owner to specify which system software (operating systems) are allowed to perform a measured launch and also prevent an allowed OS/VMM from performing a measured launch if its trusted code has been altered. Remember that the code that is measured and executed first after the SENTER is referred to as the *measured launch environment* (MLE) measurement.

There is an expectation that the TBOOT MLE code will first enable and enforce all of the protections mechanisms, after which it will then load, measure, and authenticate additional modules (such as kernel code and drivers). An OS can use the fact that MLE code passing LCP means that it has not been altered, and thus data objects within that code can be trusted. An example of this is when the OSV/VMV signs the kernel and other modules and includes the public signing key(s) in the MLE code. The MLE code uses the keys to verify that the kernel and other modules are authentic, and thus will not execute those modules if they have been modified or signed by the wrong key. Note that the public keys can be trusted if, and only if, the MLE code has not been modified (that is, has passed LCP).

Therefore, *whether the operating system will be trusted is determined by the measurement of its MLE code.* Each list in the policy data structure may contain an MLE element, which contains a list of MLE measurements that meet the datacenter's policy.

To include an MLE element, in the policy generator tool, select *Add MLE* and the tool will display MLE information, as illustrated in Figure 3-11. Next select the hash files to include. Hash files are provided by the OSV/VMV. The policy generator extracts the MLE hash from the file such that the policy data structure only contains the hash values (not file names). The MLE policy also allows you to specify the minimum SINIT version that can be used to launch those OS/VMMs specified in that list.

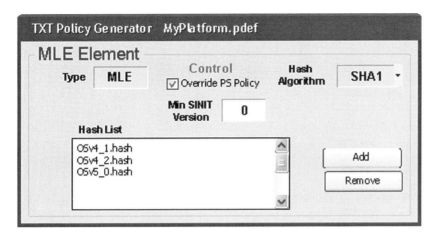

Figure 3-11. *MLE policy generator*

At the time of the measured launch, the policy engine evaluates the MLE policy, comparing that actual MLE measurement to those in the MLE elements until it finds a match. If there is no MLE policy (no MLE element in the policy data structure), then the MLE policy equates to TRUE. If the MLE measurement matches one of the measurements in the MLE Element, then the MLE policy evaluates to TRUE. Otherwise (no match), the MLE policy evaluates to FALSE, which results in a TXT reset.

Specifying Trusted ACMs

Regardless of how much an ACM is tested, there is still a possibility of security vulnerabilities. Even more important, ACMs can be updated with enhanced security checking and other features. As with any software, ACMs mature over time, and thus the launch control policy provides for the platform owner to specify the minimum version of the SINIT ACM that will be allowed to perform a measured launch. This is done in order to prevent malicious software from replacing the ACM with an older ACM to take advantage of a known flaw or shortcoming. It should be noted that Intel has its own means to revoke both BIOS ACMs and SINIT ACMs if the need arises, and that means does not involve the LCP (it uses NVRAM controlled by the ACMs to store the revocation values). Thus, revoking ACMs because of security flaws are handled regardless of the LCP.

There are actually two ways to set the minimum SINIT version. Both the MLE element in the policy data structure and the NV policy data contain a "minimum SINIT version," and whichever is larger determines the minimum value for the platform. The value in the NV policy data allows the platform owner to establish the minimum for all policies. The value in the MLE element applies to the measurements listed in that element, and thus the platform owner can specify different minimums for different OS/VMMs. Although I am not sure how practical this is, the capability is there. The real value is that using the min SINIT in a signed list avoids having to update the TPM NVRAM.

Specifying a Policy of "ANY"

The platform owner can specify a launch control policy of ANY. This means that the policy does not provide PCONF or MLE measurements, and thus any OS/VMM on any platform configuration is permitted to perform a measured launch. This is an acceptable policy, especially when there is remote attestation. However, remote attestation applies its policy after the measured launch.

Since there are no PCONF and MLE elements, there is no need for the policy data structure. Thus, the NV policy data contains all of the information needed for the ACM to evaluate the launch control policy.

Revoking Platform Default Policy

The platform supplier also provides an NV policy data and (optionally) a policy data structure that affect the measured launch. Unlike the platform owner policy (PO policy), the platform supplier policy (PS policy—sometimes referred to as *platform default* or *PD policy*) may contain an SBIOS element that is used by a different policy engine to protect against reset attacks. The owner policy has no impact with respect to the SBIOS policy. Typically, the platform supplier policy is set to ANY (that is, does not contain PCONF or MLE elements) unless there is one of the following:

- *A fallback BIOS.* The platform supplier has the capability to switch back to the original BIOS image (in case the current BIOS/VMM becomes corrupted). Thus the PS policy contains an SBIOS element that specifies the measurement of the original BIOS startup code.

- *A signed BIOS policy.* The platform supplier has the capability to gracefully switch to another BIOS image (in case of BIOS update or falling back to a previous version). The PS policy contains an SBIOS element specifying measurements of authorized BIOS startup code, signed by the vendor, so it can be updated as part of the BIOS update.

- *A preinstalled OS/VMM:* The platform ships with an OS/VMM installed. The supplier may optionally provide PCONF and MLE elements.

The presence of the SBIOS element does not influence the launch control policy for the measured launch. If the platform does not come with a preinstalled OS/VMM, then typically there are no PCONF or MLE elements in the PS policy, and as far as the launch control policy engine is concerned, the PS policy is the same as ANY. Even when the platform does come with a preinstalled OS/VMM, the platform supplier is not required to include PCONF and MLE elements. But let's consider what happens when the PS policy does contain either PCONF or MLE elements.

The PCONF element and MLE element in the PO policy each have a flag that can be set to override the corresponding PS policy element. If the override flag is not set, then that policy evaluates to TRUE if either the PO policy element or the PS policy element evaluates TRUE. When the override flag is set, the policy engine does not evaluate the corresponding element in the PS policy. Table 3-1 shows how the SINT ACM interprets the policies.

Table 3-1. *Policy Significance*

PO Policy	PS Policy	Result
None	ANY	Any PCONF & any MLE
	Only PCONF	PS.PCONF & any MLE
	PCONF&MLE	PS.PCONF & PS.MLE
	Only MLE	Any PCONF & PS.MLE
ANY	<don't care>	Any PCONF & any MLE
Only PCONF	ANY	PO.PCONF & any MLE
	Only PCONF	(PO.PCONF+PS.PCONF) & any MLE
	PCONF&MLE	
	Only MLE	PO.PCONF & any MLE
PCONF+MLE	ANY	PO.PCONF & PO.MLE
	Only PCONF	(PO.PCONF+PS.PCONF) & PO.MLE
	PCONF&MLE	(PO.PCONF+PS.PCONF) & (PO.MLE+PS.MLE)
	Only MLE	PO.PCONF & (PO.MLE+PS.MLE)

(continued)

Table 3-1. (*continued*)

PO Policy	PS Policy	Result
Only MLE	ANY	Any PCONF & PO.MLE
	Only PCONF	
	PCONF&MLE	Any PCONF & (PO.MLE+PS.MLE)
	Only MLE	
PCONF (override)	<don't care>	PO.PCONF & any MLE
PCONF (override) & MLE	ANY	PO.PCONF & PO.MLE
	Only PCONF	
	PCONF&MLE	PO.PCONF & (PO.MLE+PS.MLE)
	Only MLE	
PCONF & MLE (override)	ANY	PO.PCONF & PO.MLE
	Only PCONF	(PO.PCONF+PS.PCONF) & PO.MLE
	PCONF&MLE	
	Only MLE	PO.PCONF & PO.MLE
PCONF (override) & MLE (override)	<don't care>	PO.PCONF & PO.MLE
MLE (override)	<don't care>	Any PCONF & PO.MLE

■ **Note** A "+" means if either equates true, "&" means both must equate true, "none" means either the policy does not exist or the policy is not ANY and there are neither PCONF nor MLE elements.

Why Is PO Policy Important?

Most likely when you install a new platform, measured launch works without having to create a platform owner policy. So let's look at some reasons why it is beneficial for you to do so.

■ **Note** Before publishing this book, we asked a few leading datacenter managers to review its content. According to feedback from a senior datacenter technologist, this entire section deserves to be highlighted. So we thought we would convey his emphasis to you. Also, we would like to thank those who did review, and thus helped make this a better book.

Prevent Interference by the Platform Supplier Policy

The platform vendor providing a preinstalled OS/VMM means well by providing a PS policy with the OS/VMM measurement. This was done as an aid in providing the initial policy with the expectation that the datacenter will supplement it with the PO policy.

As you can see from Table 3-1 and Figure 3-8, if there is no PO policy and there is a PS policy for a preinstalled OS/VMM, then the PS policy can prevent a measured launch after the datacenter either updates the BIOS or updates the OS/VMM. The solution to this problem is to create a platform owner policy, even if that policy is ANY.

Establishing Trusted Pools

The owner policy is the place where the datacenter asserts its policy on what is considered "trusted." The fact that a platform has performed a secure launch attests to the platform complying with prescribed procedures for protecting the OS/VMM and its data. For instance, when an OS boots, all of the processors are started in *real* mode, and the OS has to transition them to *virtual* mode and then to *protected* mode. During this time, there are vulnerabilities. To negate those vulnerabilities, the measured launch places all the processors in a special sleep state and wakes them up in protected mode—but only after the initiating processor has set up all of the protections.

Thus performing the measured launch is sufficient qualification for a server platform to be considered part of a trusted pool of servers. However, the datacenter might want to impose additional requirements or otherwise qualify what is considered "trusted." That can be enforced via the platform owner policy, as illustrated in Figure 3-12.

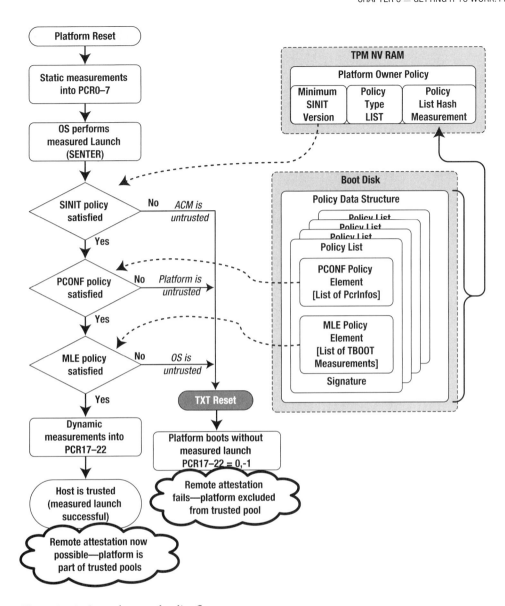

Figure 3-12. *Launch control policy flow*

Let's take a look at an example. Referring to the MLE policy in Figure 3-13, assume an older version of the OS (version 4.x in our example) has a known vulnerability, and even though that version is capable of performing a measured launch, you want to exclude it from the pool of trusted servers.

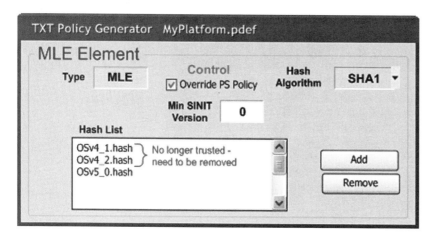

Figure 3-13. *MLE policy generator*

The solution is to create a policy that includes the measurements of only the trusted versions. So we simply remove the measurements for version 4.1 and 4.2. Any platforms with the older OS/VMM versions are now prevented from performing a measured launch, and thus prevented from joining the pool of trusted servers (at least until their OS is updated)—this is because attestation will fail since PCR17 and 18 will contain all zeros.

As you update the OS/VMM on the untrusted servers, those servers will now pass the measured launch control policy, and thus once again join the pool of trusted servers. Once all servers have been updated, you might be tempted to change the policy back to ANY, but that would not protect against an attack where malicious software was able to roll back the OS/VMM version to take advantage of its vulnerability.

Reduce the Need for Remote Attestation

To determine if a platform has passed the launch control policy, all that needs to be done is to verify that PCR18 contains a nonzero value. For those who trust the datacenter to establish a launch control policy that meets their needs, this should be sufficient. Otherwise, remote attestation will need to compare PCR values with lists of known good values.

At this point, we should discuss the difference between private clouds and public clouds. One of the biggest drivers for remote attestation is the ability to satisfy the service client about the integrity of the platform that is hosting the client's applications. This is a significant factor for public clouds (where the service clients are not part of the organization providing the computing services).

But what about private clouds (where the service provider and service clients are part of the same organization)? In this case, the datacenter would be trusted with maintaining the integrity of the services without the need for remote attestation by a third party. Thus the establishment and use of trusted pools might very well be sufficient for the service clients, and therefore the satisfaction of the platform owner policy provides the level of attestation required by the clients.

One could also extend this argument to include a public cloud provider providing services for clients within its own organization. I can imagine that the billing department for Amazon.com would trust its own organization to provide secure services, while the billing department for an external client would want an audit trail confirmed by a third party via remote attestation. There would be no need to burden a client within the service provider's organization with overhead for remote attestation. On the other hand, if remote attestation is there, why not make use of it?

Reset Attack Protection

One of the benefits of Intel TXT is protection against reset attacks. A reset attack is where an attacker causes a platform reset before the OS/VMM can do an orderly shutdown. Thus there can be secrets such as encryption keys, passwords, and personal information left unprotected in memory.

To negate reset attacks, Intel TXT maintains a *Secrets* flag, which the OS/VMM sets after it does a measured launch, but before placing any secrets in memory. The OS/VMM clears the *Secrets* flag when it does a graceful shutdown (after removing all secrets and sensitive information from memory). If the platform resets before the *Secrets* flag is cleared, the memory must be scrubbed. For client platforms, the memory architecture is simple, so the ACM performs the memory scrubbing and does not enable memory controllers until after it has scrubbed the memory. Since the memory architecture for servers is more complex, the ACM has to depend on the BIOS to scrub the memory. When the *Secrets* flag is set when the platform initializes, the memory controllers are disabled until the BIOS ACM validates that the BIOS is trusted to scrub memory. This is where the SBIOS policy engine comes into play.

There are two types of SBIOS policy. The platform vendor may choose either autopromotion (the most common at this time) or signed BIOS policy (which is receiving a lot of interest from manufacturers):

- *Autopromotion.* Each time the platform resets, the BIOS ACM measures the BIOS startup (SBIOS) code and places that measurement in a TPM NVRAM location to remember it for the next boot. If the platform performs a measured launch, it means that the PCONF policy was satisfied, and thus the BIOS was trusted. If the platform resets with secrets in memory (that is, the *Secrets* flag set), then the SBIOS policy engine measures the BIOS startup code and makes sure it had not been altered. It does this by comparing its measurement against the saved measurement.

- *Signed BIOS policy.* Instead of using the remembered SBIOS measurement, when the platform resets with the *Secrets* bit set, the SBIOS policy engine compares the measurement of the BIOS startup code to a list of measurements signed by the platform vendor. Because the list is signed, each BIOS update can provide a new signed list of SBIOS measurements for the current code.

Signed BIOS policy is independent of launch control policy. That is, for the BIOS to be trusted, its measurement must match the known good value provided by the factory. On the other hand, autopromotion depends on the LCP to determine if the BIOS is trusted.

Therefore, after a reset attack, the malicious software finds nothing in memory. And an attempt to alter the BIOS to bypass the scrubbing will result in no memory. There is a weakness with autopromotion that can be mitigated with the PO policy. If LCP allows any platform configuration, then any BIOS corruption that occurs before the last platform reset would not be detected. This can easily be avoided by setting a PO PCONF policy that uses the PCR0 measurement. Now, PCR0 must contain a known good value and because the PCR0 value includes the SBIOS measurement, any corruption to the BIOS prevents the measured launch.

Considerations

There are a number of issues to consider when establishing the launch control policy.

- The launch control policy consists of setting MLE policy, PCONF policy, and SINIT policy.

- Changing SINIT policy can be done by changing the TPM NV policy data or changing the MLE element in the policy data structure. Changing the NV policy data requires performing a privileged TPM operation on each platform.

- Changing MLE policy or PCONF policy can be done without changing the NV policy data if the platform owner uses signed policies. Signed policies allow the datacenter to push policy updates "down the wire," making it easier to administer launch control policies. See "Policy Management" in the next chapter.

- MLE policy uses the measurement of the TBOOT MLE code to verify that the code has not been altered by comparing the measurement to a list of known good values. Each OS/VMM update potentially adds another known good value. An OS/VMM version/revision number should be part of the TBOOT MLE code to force a new measurement for each major update. Without this, the LCP will not be able to distinguish between different versions of the software (if there are no updates to the TBOOT MLE code). The platform owner needs to know if the TBOOT MLE measurement implicitly changes with each update or just major updates.

- The downside of including a revision value in the TBOOT MLE measurement is that every revision requires updating the PO policy. See "MLE Updates" under "Policy Management" in the next chapter.

- PCONF is the set of measurements that defines the platform configuration. PCR0 contains the static root of trust for the other static PCRs (PCR 1–7). PCR0 should always be included because PCR0 attests to the integrity of the other PCR measurements.

- PCR0 contains multiple measurements, but, in essence, it represents the BIOS code. Including PCR0 in the PCONF policy verifies that the code was provided by the factory (at the time the platform left the factory or the BIOS update as sent from the factory). Any change to any part of the BIOS trusted code results in a change to the PCR0 measurement. Thus, including PCR0 detects any unauthorized BIOS changes.

- The downside of including PCR0 in the PCONF policy is that every BIOS update requires updating the PO policy. See "BIOS Updates" under "Policy Management" in the next chapter.

- There is an inherent complexity in using multiple PCRs in the PCONF policy. That is, the combinations of PCRInfos that need to be specified multiply with the number of variations. For example, let's say the PCONF policy uses PCR0, PCR1, and PCR4, and there are three acceptable values for PCR0, four for PCR1, and two for PCR4. This would require 3×4×2=24 PCRInfos to allow all combinations. A BIOS update that adds another PCR0 value changes that to 4×4×2=32—meaning eight more PCRInfos must be added to the policy. On the other hand, if the new PCR0 value replaces one of the others, then eight of the original PCRInfos would have to be removed. This requires sophisticated policy management tools to simplify policy tracking.

Summary

At this point, you should have a good understanding of what needs to be done to enable Intel TXT from BIOS setup, establishing TPM ownership, and installing system software. These are very objective steps, and although they do vary from vendor to vendor, the learning curve is simple and you should be able to get specific information directly from the platform manufacturer as well as the OS/VMM vendor.

On the other hand, launch control policy is very subjective and depends more on the datacenter and the availability of tools for creating, setting, and maintaining policies. The next chapter will walk you through the process for selecting a launch control policy that meets your needs.

■ ■ ■

CHAPTER 4

Foundation for Control: Establishing Launch Control Policy

Now it is time to discuss which launch control policies are right for your datacenter. That decision rests on many factors and the purpose of this chapter is to help you understand those tradeoffs. We will also discuss how to manage policies, because setting the policy for one machine is not hard, but managing a datacenter with hundreds of servers can be challenging. Managing tens of thousands of servers requires quite a bit of discipline.

Quick Review of Launch Control Policy

In the previous chapter, we established that the launch control policy consisted of three independent policies, as illustrated in Figure 4-1.

- *SINIT policy* prevents a measured launch using an older SINIT Authenticated Code Module (ACM). This is done by specifying the minimum ACM version that is allowed to perform the measured launch. The minimum SINIT version is specified in the NV policy data stored in the TPM NVRAM and may also be specified in an MLE policy element (in the policy data structure).

- *Platform Configuration (PCONF) policy* prevents a measured launch unless the platform configuration matches a known good configuration, as measured by the values in a set of PCRs selected by you. These known good configurations are listed in a *PCONF policy element* that is part of the policy data structure stored in the boot directory.

- *MLE policy* prevents a measured launch unless the OS/VMM measurement matches a known good value. These known good measurements are listed in an MLE policy element that is part of the policy data structure.

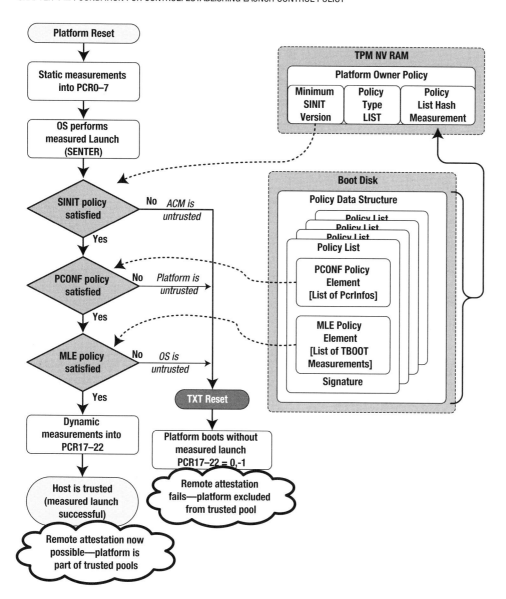

Figure 4-1. *Overview of launch control policy*

You may select a policy type of ANY or LIST. With a policy type of ANY, you can still enforce SINIT policy while allowing any OS/VMM to perform a measured launch using any platform configuration.

With a policy type of LIST, you can specifically establish a platform configuration policy, MLE policy, or both by specifying lists of known good values.

The lists of known good values reside on disk in a policy data file, and to prevent tampering, the policy type and the measurement of the policy file are stored in (and protected by) the TPM's NVRAM.

When Is Launch Control Policy Needed?

In the previous chapter, we raised the following questions:

- Is remote attestation needed if there is a strong launch control policy?

- Is a launch control policy needed if there is remote attestation?

These answers are very subjective, will vary from datacenter to datacenter, and most likely will vary over time. To discuss those questions, we need a better understanding of remote attestation.

Remote Attestation

In a nutshell, *remote attestation* makes policy decisions based on the server's integrity as measured by its PCR values (illustrated in Figure 4-2). But wait, isn't this what the launch control policy does?

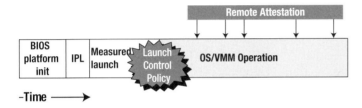

Figure 4-2. *Policy decisions*

The answer is yes and no. Yes, the LCP makes a policy decision based on the PCR measurements. But LCP controls the ability of the platform to do a measured launch and prevents untrusted platforms from performing the measured launch. Remote attestation cannot control the measured launch because it uses the PCR values derived from the measured launch. On the other hand, remote attestation can impact many other decision processes and can govern the operation of the platform. For example, it could do the following:

- Determine if a platform is trusted and cause an untrusted platform to be placed into quarantine, isolating it from the hive, and denying it access to storage and the production network.

- Establish various levels of trust based on both the platform and the OS/VMM version.

- Determine which applications (if any) are allowed to run on which servers. In later chapters, we will look at how trust-based migration policies control whether an application is allowed to migrate to another platform that has a different trust level.

- Assure compliance with government and corporate regulations.

- Provide an audit trail that can prove compliance to both customer and government requirements.

The implementation and usage of remote attestation is very flexible. Thus, there can be very few or many agents involved in remote attestation, such as agents that pull measurements from the servers, an agent that evaluates those measurements against known good values (white lists) to establish a trust level, and various management agents that each enforce policies based on that determination. Essentially, there are very few limits on what can be done with remote attestation.

What Does Launch Control Policy Deliver?

It's useful to think of launch control policy as the precursor to remote attestation. That is, LCP is the first level of defense that occurs at boot-time, and remote attestation is the second level that occurs as often as needed. Here are some capabilities of launch control policy that remote attestation does not provide:

- *Enhanced protection against reset attacks.* When the BIOS uses autopromotion, the defense relies on the LCP to determine if the BIOS is trusted in the first place. With a policy of ANY, the platform is protected against alteration/corruption of BIOS after the last boot (and before the reset), but cannot protect against long-term corruption (that is, before the last boot). Using a PCONF policy detects any BIOS corruption. If the BIOS uses a signed SBIOS policy, then this is not an issue because the OEM provides the list of known good SBIOS measurements. Remember that SBIOS is the trusted portion of BIOS responsible for mitigating the reset attack. Thus, at the time of a reset attack, the platform detects a corrupted SBIOS regardless of when the corruption occurred. Although signed BIOS policy is ideal for protection against reset attacks, it does not replace the PCONF policy in the LCP. That is because the signed BIOS policy only comes into play after the reset attack and the PCONF policy is evaluated at every launch (typically as part of loading the OS/VMM).

- *Restrict TPM access.* Any OS/VMM has access to TPM locality 0, however, only an OS/VMM that passes the launch control policy has access to TPM locality 2. Locality 2 is what gives the OS/VMM the ability to measure its components into the dynamic PCRs (19–22) and thus seal/unseal data to those values. Likewise, keys, TPM NVRAM, and other TPM resources can be tied to locality 2, preventing anyone except the trusted OS/VMM from using them. By using a stronger launch control policy (specifically an MLE policy), you further prevent rogue software from impersonating a trusted OS/VMM, and thus further restrict what software can even attempt to use those protected resources.

- *Self-contained.* Although remote attestation is more flexible, it does bring additional complexity that is not always needed. For example, consider a private cloud scenario where the service clients implicitly trust their IT department and have no need for third-party, trust-based compliance and auditing. For this case, the local attestation provided by the launch control policy is all that is needed.

The bottom line is that launch control policy is applied before the OS/VMM is permitted to do a measured launch and remote attestation comes sometime later.

It is possible that over time, remote attestation capability will grow to the point where the value of launch control policy diminishes. For example, consider a device that evaluates the platform's measurements immediately after the launch and either quarantines the platform or powers it down. This could be just as effective as failing the launch control policy, especially if this is done before any applications are allowed to execute. For this case, the autopromotion requirement would be satisfied because the protection from the early remote attestation would be as effective as the TXT reset caused by LCP.

Let's review one more thought before we get down to the details of selecting the policy components. That is, full-blown remote attestation takes the platform's PCR measurements and compares them to known good values, and then uses that result to determine a trust level. The final role is for a management application to make a policy-based decision using that trust level. So, if the platforms provide an adequate launch control policy, it might be sufficient for the management application just to detect that the platform was able to perform a measured launch. Now much of the complexity of remote attestation goes away, because management applications only need to detect whether PCR18 contains the default value—any other value indicates that the platform passed the launch control policy.

Platform Configuration (PCONF) Policy

Before you can decide if you want to specify a PCONF policy as part of your launch control policy, you need a better understanding of what it means to specify a PCONF policy and how you can customize the PCONF policy.

The biggest problem with having a PCONF policy is that there is no single correct policy, and most likely the best-suited policy for you this year will not be the best in the years to come.

One other thought to keep in mind is that, as mentioned in Chapter 1, Intel® Trusted Execution Technology is part of a defense-in-depth strategy. BIOS developers have incorporated many security concepts (such as signed BIOS updates and password-protected configuration) that protect against malicious BIOS corruption and unauthorized platform configuration change. PCONF policy is yet another layer of protection. The other side of the coin is that there are additional advantages that can be derived from a PCONF policy. The point is that as you evaluate what PCONF policy to use, also consider protections offered by other technologies.

Specifying Trusted Platform Configurations

The first step in creating the PCONF portion of the launch control policy is to determine the matrix of PCRs (that is, which PCRs need to be examined). In the previous chapter, we identified that PCR0–PCR7 were candidates and that part of the PCONF policy is selecting which PCRs to include, as illustrated in Figure 4-3.

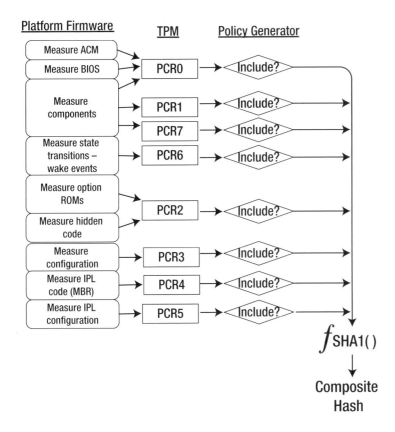

Figure 4-3. *PCONF PCR selection*

So let's take a closer look.

PCR0: CRTM, BIOS, and Host Platform Extensions

You will always want to include PCR0 because it contains the core-root-of-trust (CRTM), and thus it attests to the validity of the other PCRs. In addition, this PCR value represents the BIOS integrity. If the BIOS has been corrupted or maliciously altered, it will show up in this measurement. Here is what the TCG requires[1] being measured into PCR0:

- The CRTM's version identifier.

- All firmware physically bound to the motherboard.

- Manufacturer-controlled embedded option ROMs. These are embedded option ROMs whose release and updates are controlled by the platform manufacturer.

- Embedded System Management Module (SMM) code and the code that sets it up.

- ACPI flash data prior to any modifications.

- Boot Integrity Service (BIS) code (excluding the BIS certificate).

The TCG specification also requires that "If the measurement of the CRTM, POST BIOS and Embedded Option ROMs cannot be made, the CRTM MUST extend the value 01h to each PCR in the range 0–7." This prevents rogue code from extending those PCRs with what would appear to be known good values.

The TCG allows the BIOS to measure "any other code or information that is relevant to the CRTM, POST BIOS or Platform Extensions" to PCR0. Typically, all BIOS code gets measured to PCR0 because OEMs want the maximum coverage and don't want to risk their reputation by excluding a piece of code that could be the target of an attack.

> *Unauthorized modification of BIOS firmware by malicious software constitutes a significant threat because of the BIOS's unique and privileged position within the PC architecture. A malicious BIOS modification could be part of a sophisticated, targeted attack on an organization—either a permanent denial of service (if the BIOS is corrupted) or a persistent malware presence (if the BIOS is implanted with malware).*
>
> —NIST: National Institute of Standards and Technology, US Department of Commerce, Special Publication 800-147 *BIOS Protection Guidelines*

It is easy to see why including PCR0 should be fundamental. If the BIOS code is altered, either accidentally or maliciously, the platform could experience loss of confidentiality, integrity, and availability—resulting in system instability, system failure, and/or information leakage.

PCR1: Host Platform Configuration

This is the second most important PCR because it can be used to detect unauthorized changes to BIOS configuration. Unauthorized changes to platform configuration can potentially be just as disruptive and threatening as changes to BIOS code because it also could cause system instability, system failure, and/or information leakage.

The TCG requires the following components be measured into PCR1:

- CPU microcode update

- Platform configuration, including the state of any *disable flags* affecting the measurement of entities into this PCR

---

[1]From the *TCG PC Specific Implementation Specification*, Version 1.1, August 18, 2003, Copyright© 2003 Trusted Computing Group, Incorporated.

- BIS certificate (measurement can be disabled)

- POST BIOS-based ROM strings (measurement can be disabled)

The TCG allows measurement of the following (excluding privacy information):

- ESCD, CMOS, and other NVRAM data

- SMBIOS structures

- Passwords

BIOS does not measure values that are dynamic, such as counters, system time/date, or anything else that automatically changes. This means that the PCR1 measurement should be the same from boot to boot if there is no configuration change. It also excludes system-unique information, such as asset numbers and serial numbers. Thus, identical platforms configured the same should produce the same PCR0 and PCR1 values.

It was discovered that not all manufactures initially realized this requirement, so some platforms out there will not have the same PCR0 and PCR1 values, even when they are configured identically. If you have any of these platforms, it is not a security concern, but it will require additional effort to include them in a global PCONF policy. This has been corrected, and as of 2012, all manufactures were conforming to this requirement.

PCR2, 3: Option ROM Code and Configuration Data

Since option ROMs provide the means for add-in cards to provide firmware extensions (especially for adding boot capabilities), this PCR provides additional protection for platforms that contain plug-in devices that impact the boot flow. This can include option ROMs on the main board that are not controlled by the BIOS update.

It's prudent to be a little skeptical about PCR3. We know we can trust the BIOS to measure the visible portion of the option ROM code into PCR2; however, the visible option ROM code is responsible for measuring any hidden portions of the code (and extending into PCR2), as well as measuring device configuration information and extending that measurement into PCR3. The authors are not aware of any program that actually confirms that I/O device vendors adhere to those requirements. Therefore, it would not be surprising if PCR3 never gets extended by the I/O device. Check with the device manufacturer to see whether the device complies with TCG requirements.

Even if this is the case, it doesn't mean you should not specify PCR3; rather it means that the effectiveness of specifying PCR3 may be reduced, so you will only want to purchase add-on devices that comply with TCG requirements.

The importance of including PCR2 (and PCR3) in the PCONF policy depends on a number of factors:

- If there are never any add-in cards, then this becomes a "don't care." Adding PCR2 to PCONF policy would be a way to detect if an I/O card is added (or removed). On the other hand, do you want such an event to prevent measured launch (until a card is removed/replaced or PCONF policy is updated)? Note that add-in devices that don't have option ROMs have no impact and are not a concern because they don't impact the boot flow and they don't show up in the PCR2 and PCR3 measurements.

- If any of the add-in cards can impact the boot choice, and the MLE policy is ANY (meaning no MLE element), then including these PCRs can provide additional protection against attacks seeking to load a different OS/VMM.

- Once the OS boots, it typically installs its own (signed) I/O drivers, and thus does not depend on option ROM code or configuration. If this is the case, and the MLE policy only allows authenticated OS/VMM, then the value of detecting option ROM modifications is reduced.

- Many option ROMs are implemented using flash memory so that they can be updated. Option ROM updates don't get the same level of scrutiny as BIOS updates. Including PCR2 or PCR3 in PCONF policy means that anytime there is an option ROM update, the PCONF policy must be updated. Since the OS handles driver updates, you might not be aware that the update takes place until the measured launch fails.

- Don't forget that any option ROM is a potential attack point. That is, if malicious software can control the flash image, it can configure the option ROM to insert itself into the boot process—regardless of the functionality of the original code.

PCR4, 5: IPL Code and Configuration Data

These two PCRs can be used to assure that you boot from the same source. PCR4 contains the measurement of the initial program loader (IPL) code. Typically, this comes from the master boot record (MBR) when booting via a storage device or the bootstrap code from the network. By definition, it is the code that performs the handoff from the BIOS to the OS. What makes PCR4 potentially difficult to use is that each time the BIOS selects a boot device, it measures the IPL code, and if the code returns to the BIOS to find another device, the BIOS measures the IPL code of the next device. Since measurements are extended and not replaced, the final value of PCR4 depends on the order in which boot attempts are made. Thus you will always want to place your primary boot source first in the boot priority. Also remember that booting from a CD/DVD or from a USB will produce different digests, and you will want to make sure to include those if you need to boot a "trusted OS" by multiple methods.

The authors are not aware of any OS/VMM installation/reinstallation that requires a secure launch. So this is not likely a consideration—if you run into such a problem you will need to change the policy. Consider setting LCP=ANY during the installation and then resuming with PCONF policy.

PCR 5 holds the measurement of any configuration data that the IPL code might need (such as disk geometry). In many cases, there is no additional data needed (such as booting from a single partition disk). Also, it is the IPL code, not the BIOS, that extends the configuration data into PCR5. Thus, if the IPL code is not TCG compliant or there is no additional configuration data, this PCR may not be very useful.

PCR6: State Transition and Wake Events

This PCR gets extended by both the BIOS and the OS. The BIOS extends this register on wake events and the OS extends it on power state change. Here are the expected actions (per ACPI power state):

- *S0*: Normal operation, platform fully operational.

- *S1*: Standby w/ Low latency wakeup. This is typical of the platform reducing the processor clock rate to save power. TPM remains powered so PCR values are preserved. This can happen automatically without OS or BIOS knowledge. All contexts are maintained. The chain of trust is not broken, and thus nothing is extended to PCR6 upon entering or exiting this state.

- *S2*: Standby with CPU context lost. This is typical of an OS-involved, reduced-power state taking one or more cores offline during idle periods. BIOS is not involved and the TPM remains powered so PCR values are preserved. All other contexts are maintained. The chain of trust is not broken, and thus nothing is extended to PCR6 upon entering or exiting this state.

- *S3*: Suspend to RAM. This is where the OS calls the BIOS to put the platform in a deep sleep state, preserving RAM contents but powering down other components, including the TPM. The TPM is instructed to save its state, which includes the PCR values. When the platform wakes, the BIOS ACM detects that the platform is waking from S3 and restarts the TPM, causing it to reload the original PCR values. The chain of trust is interrupted but not broken as long as the resume is successful. The OS (optionally) extends PCR6 with the TPM_SaveState event immediately before entering S3, and when successfully resuming from S3, the BIOS ACM extends PCR6 with the TPM_ResumeState.

- *S4*: Suspend to disk. This is where the OS saves its context to disk and powers down the platform. When the platform wakes from S4, it goes through a normal startup and loads the OS, which recovers its previous state from disk and resumes where it left off. BIOS and TPM don't do anything special when waking from S4. Thus the chain of trust terminates on entering S4, and upon waking from S4, all PCRs are reset to their initial values and the chain of trust is rebuilt. There is no need to extend anything to PCR6 on entering or exiting S4, because the PCR will be reset.

- *S5*: Power OFF. This is where the OS simply powers down the platform (or power is lost, or the platform is reset). When the platform wakes from S5, it goes through a normal startup. BIOS and TPM don't do anything special when waking from S5. Thus the chain of trust terminates on entering S5, and upon waking from S5, all PCRs are reset to their initial values and the chain of trust is rebuilt. There is no need to extend anything to PCR6 on entering or exiting S5, because the PCR will be reset.

Including PCR6 in the PCONF policy is not very useful for servers. Server platforms don't support S3, and the PCR6 value does not change for the other power states. Workstations do support S3; however, workstations are outside the authors' area of expertise and we cannot offer any insight on the value of PCR6 for a workstation's PCONF policy.

PCR7: Host Platform Manufacturer Control

The content of this PCR is not currently defined and reserved for the platform manufacturer. Unless you know what is being measured into this PCR, you should not include it in the PCONF Policy.

Tools Needed for Creating a PCONF Policy

The primary tool will be the LCP policy generator, as described in the previous chapter. You will also need a tool that can gather the needed PCR values for input to the LPC policy generator, such as PcrDump. PcrDump is a tool that executes on the target platform, reads the values in all PCRs, and saves them to a file. You may want to consider naming the file after the platform and BIOS version (example: DellR410v18.pcr). You only need to do this once for each group of platforms that will have identical PCR values. That is, all identical platforms with the same BIOS version are considered a group. Copy the PCR dump file to the working directory for the policy generator. When you run the policy generator tool, specify which PCRs you want to include, plus the PCR dump file name(s), and the tool generates the PCONF policy element by creating a PCRInfo structure for each PCR file specified, as illustrated in Figure 4-4.

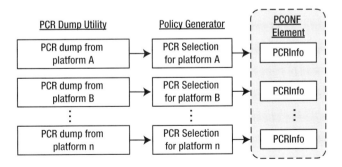

Figure 4-4. *Building the PCONF element*

The PCRInfo is simply a structure that identifies which PCRs were selected, and contains a composite hash digest created by hashing the selected PCR values. When the policy engine executes, it reads each PCRInfo to determine which PCRs to evaluate, performs a hash of those selected PCRs (using the current value from the TPM), and compares that digest to the composite hash digest in the PCRInfo. The digest will only match if all of the selected PCRs' values in the TPM are the same as the corresponding values in the PcrDump file used to create the PCRInfo.

The LPC policy generator builds a policy list that includes that PCONF policy element and provides the means for you to sign that list (you specify the key file that contains the public and private signing keys). The final step is for the LPC generator to generate the policy data structure and the NV policy data (for the portion of the policy that is stored in the TPM NVRAM, which contains the measurement of the policy data structure).

You will need a different tool for updating the TPM NVRAM (if necessary; see the discussion on using signed policy lists later in this chapter). That capability is typically provided by the OS/VMM (if the OS/VMM is the TPM owner) or by the management software you used to establish TPM ownership.

Difficulties with Using PCONF Policy

Hopefully by now you have a good idea of which PCRs you want to include in your ideal PCONF policy. PCR0 should be one of them (and possibly the only one). But there are challenges with specifying a PCONF policy.

As we stated in the previous chapter, one of the biggest challenges in maintaining a policy that includes PCR0 is that each BIOS update changes the value in PCR0. Thus, the PCONF policy must be updated to include the new "known good" value.

Here's the catch: if you update the BIOS before you update the policy, then the platform will fail its measured launch. To update the policy before the BIOS update, you must already know the new PCR value. Some solutions follow.

One solution is to update the machine offline (where it is not vulnerable) with a policy of ANY (or don't perform a measured launch), capture the new PCR values, update the policy, and push the policy to all platforms that will get that BIOS update. You will need to make sure you keep the old platform configuration in the PCONF policy to permit platforms to continue to launch before the BIOS update and to allow fallback in case the BIOS update fails.

Another solution is for the OS/VMM to perform a sanity check before it does a measured launch. The sanity check consists of testing if the policy is satisfied. If not, it notifies the user and prompts the user to accept the configuration change. If the user selects "accept," the OS prompts for authorization to accept the change (example: the TPM password or system administrator's password). This sanity check works for any platform configuration change. The tool simply looks at the existing PCRInfo to determine which PCRs the platform owner had selected, and uses that set of PCRs for both the sanity check and the PCONF policy update. For this case, each BIOS update (or any change to the platform configuration) results in a simple authenticated acknowledgement.

Unfortunately, we don't know of any OS/VMM that currently implements that capability. Perhaps you might want to talk to your favorite OS/VMM vendor about the value of providing such a capability.

Another potential solution (when only PCR0 integrity is needed) comes from relying on the PS policy (the one that the platform manufacturer provides). Many OEMs are planning on using signed BIOS policy, which allows them to provide an SBIOS element containing the list of known good SBIOS measurements. It would be fairly easy for them to include a PCONF policy element that includes only PCR0 measurement(s). The great thing about this solution is that it is automatic. That is, the BIOS update includes the new PS policy data structure, which authenticates the BIOS update. All that you would need to do is include a PCONF policy element in your Platform Owner policy data structure. It doesn't even have to contain any PCRInfo because the presence of the PCONF policy element tells the policy engine that PCONF must be satisfied, and allows the PCONF policy element in the PS policy to satisfy that requirement. However, not all OEMs support signed BIOS policy, and those that do might not support this signed SBIOS+PCONF concept.

Specifying Trusted Host Operating Systems

The MLE policy is much more intuitive because it involves only a simple measurement. That is, the measurement of the OS/VMM's trusted boot (MLE) code as calculated by the SINIT ACM during the measured launch process. Even though the value measured by the ACM is extended into PCR18, it cannot be learned by reading PCR18 (remember that PCRs are extended, not written). However, it can be learned by evaluating the PCR log for PCR18. PCR logs identify what is measured into the PCRs. The first measurement extended to PCR18 is the MLE measurement. It is that first extended value that must match a value that is listed in the MLE policy element in the policy data structure.

Another option would be for the OS/VMM vendor to provide that value. This could be done a number of ways. My favorite is for the OSV/VMM to provide a default signed policy data structure that includes valid MLE measurements. Here is how that works (if supported by the OSV):

- OSV/VMV creates a policy data structure (OS PDS) that includes a single MLE policy element, which lists the valid MLE measurements—typically, only a single measurement is needed.

- When the OS/VMM is installed, the OS creates the PO policy in the TPM NVRAM specifying PolicyType = LIST and the list hash of that OS PDS.

- If you desire a policy that only includes MLE and not PCONF policy, then you do nothing; otherwise, you create the Owner PDS using the MLE policy element from the OS PDS and your own PCONF policy element. Both the OS PDS and the Owner PDS are located in the boot directory. You update the PO_POLICY data in the TPM NVRAM to specify the hash of your Owner PDS.

- When the OS does the measured launch, it uses the Owner PDS if it exists; otherwise, it uses the default PDS.

- Each OS/VMM update provides a new OS PDS containing the new list of valid MLE measurements.

  - If you have chosen to use the OS PDS, then no action is required (unless you want to revoke any previous versions).

  - Otherwise, you need to update your Owner PDS with the MLE values in the new OS PDS. If you had chosen not to use a signed list, then you also have to update the NV policy data with the new Owner PDS measurement.

Tools Needed for Creating MLE Policy

The primary tool is the LCP policy generator, as described in the previous chapter. The authors do not know of any specific tools for harvesting MLE measurements. You cannot use the PCR18 value, because the value needed for the MLE policy is the value that gets extended to PCR18, not the result after extending it. Typically, these measurements should come from the OS/VMM vendor, so check with your vendor on how they distribute that information.

The LPC policy generator builds a policy list that includes that MLE policy element and provides the means for you to sign that list (you specify the key file that contains the public and private signing keys), as illustrated in Figure 4-5. Note that if you choose to include a PCONF policy element, you may include it in the same list, or you may choose to use a different list (especially if the PCONF list is signed using a different signing key).

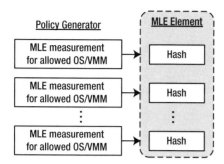

Figure 4-5. *Building the MLE element*

The final step is for the LPC generator to assemble the lists to generate the policy data structure and the NV policy data (for the portion of the policy that is stored in the TPM NVRAM, which contains the measurement of the policy data structure).

As mentioned previously, you will need a different tool for updating the TPM NVRAM, and that capability is typically provided by the OS/VMM (if the OS/VMM is the TPM owner) or by the management software that you used to establish TPM ownership.

Options and Tradeoffs

It's useful to think of launch control policy as having four parts. You are probably thinking PCONF policy, MLE policy, and SINIT policy—so what is the fourth part? Think of the PCONF policy as consisting of OEM-controlled BIOS values (PCR0) and owner-controlled configuration values (PCR1-6). The reason to do this is because BIOS updates are associated with the OEM. You might control when BIOS updates are applied, but the OEM controls the valid PCR0 values. The values for the other PCRs are controlled by actions of the datacenter and are affected by changing BIOS settings, adding/removing I/O devices, changing boot order, selecting the boot device, installing the OS/VMM, and so on.

Impact of SINIT Updates

Revocation of the SINIT ACM is rare. It happens because Intel discovers a security flaw, and that has only happened once in the history of Intel® TXT. In case of an ACM revocation, the ACMs have their own mechanism and don't rely on LCP SINIT policy. With that being said, there are other reasons for generating new versions of the SINIT ACM. Typically, it is to add or enhance features (for example, support of signed policies) or to fix a feature that didn't work as expected.

The good news is that SINIT policy is satisfied with newer SINIT ACMs. That is because ACMs are signed modules whose integrity and authenticity are validated by the processor's microcode. The only reason that you would need to change the SINIT policy is to prevent using an older SINIT. We could make guesses about why you would want to specify a SINIT policy other than *All Versions,* but the reality is that so far no one has found a need to do so. In the event that you have a reason, it requires you to take one of the following actions:

- Update the Min SINIT Version in the TPM NV policy data on each platform.

- Update the Min SINIT Version in the MLE policy element of your policy data structure. You would want to use this method if you use signed policy, because you would avoid having to modify the TPM NVRAM for each platform. However, if your MLE policy element is not in a signed list, then changing the MLE policy element requires updating the TPM NVRAM with the new hash of the policy data structure.

Impact of Platform Configuration Change

You are the only one who can predict how often you make changes to the platform configuration. Typically, it does not happen very often. In most cases, it requires taking the platform offline to perform the modification. When this does occur, you will need to update the PCONF policy element in your policy data structure, but only if you specified a PCONF that specifies more than PCR0. This will also require updating the TPM NVRAM on each platform if you don't use a signed policy list.

Impact of a BIOS Update

It's likely that BIOS updates will happen much more frequently than configuration changes. When a BIOS update does occur, you will need to update the PCONF policy element in your policy data structure (if you have one). This will also require updating the TPM NVRAM on each platform if you don't use a signed policy list.

Impact of OS/VMM Update

Typically, this happens frequently. When the OS/VMM update does occur, you will need to update the MLE policy element in your policy data structure (if you have one). This will also require updating the TPM NVRAM on each platform if you don't use a signed policy list.

Managing Launch Control Policy

It would be nice if you could just set the launch control policy and never have to touch it again. But we have seen that anytime you make a change (update the BIOS, update the OS/VMM, change the platform configuration) you need to update the policy. Dealing with one or two platforms is not a significant challenge, but dealing with hundreds or thousands of platforms from different vendors over multiple platform generations is quite challenging. Here are some tips on how you might manage them.

Think Big

It is easier to manage a single policy for all servers.

- Create the policy data structure to contain PCONF measurements for all platforms instead of managing platforms individually. Measurements are essentially unique. Thus, the probability of a measurement of a corrupted BIOS or misconfigured platform being the same as a known good measurement on a different platform can be considered nonexistent. While not required, the set of PCRs included should be the same for all platforms. This will make managing PCONF easier and allow use of PCONF management tools that automatically detect the set of PCRs that you selected. If you have a reason for using a different set of PCRs on different platforms, by all means do so.

- You might want to create multiple security domains and manage each domain separately. By security domain, we simply mean a group of servers that have a common set of security requirements and use the same set of resources including boot services. This allows you to use a different set of launch policies for each domain while using automated procedures for updating the launch control policy.

- Unless you want to prevent a particular known-good OS/VMM from launching on some platforms while allowing it to launch on others, then you can use the same MLE policy on all platforms. If you do want to enforce restricting OS/VMM on a per platform basis, then most likely you already manage servers as groups (grouped by OS/VMM). In this case, create a different policy for each group.

Use a Signed List

Using signed rather than unsigned lists allows you to update the policy without having to touch the TPM. This is because the measurement of the policy data structure has to match the measurement stored in the TPM NVRAM. The measurement of an unsigned list is the hash of the entire list. So any change to that list causes a change to the policy measurement. However, the measurement of a signed list covers just the public key that is used to verify that the list has not been compromised. Thus, updating a signed list does not change the policy measurement (as long as the list is signed with the same key).

If your servers use network boot, then all you need to do is update the policy data file on the network boot drive(s). Otherwise, use a utility to push the updated policy file to the servers.

Make Use of Vendor-Signed Policies

Make use of signed lists provided by the OS/VMM vendor. The policy data structure allows for up to eight lists and each list may be signed independently from the others. For example, you could create and sign a list that contained just a PCONF policy element, and then create the policy data structure consisting of that list and the signed list provided by the OS/VMM vendor that contains the valid MLE measurements. This would require extracting their list from their policy data structure, but that is a simple task.

Use Multiple Lists for Version Control

Consider using multiple lists for version control. Note that the reason for removing old measurements from your policy is to prevent rollback to those versions. As an example, let's say all platforms have OS/VMM version x and you want to update to version $x + 1$. You want to allow version x and $x + 1$ until you have updated all platforms. After you have updated all platforms, you wish to only allow version $x + 1$. Let's also assume that you use the signed lists provided by the OSV/VMV so you do not have to sign the MLE lists.

You initially create your policy to contain three lists—one with a PCONF policy element and two (identical) signed lists that contain an MLE policy element for version x.

When the OSV/VMV releases version $x + 1$, you replace the first signed MLE list with a new signed list for version $x + 1$ and distribute. Now both versions are allowed.

When you complete your updates, you update the policy replacing the second signed MLE list (that is, the one for version x) with another copy of the signed list for version $x + 1$. The reason that you update with a duplicate instead of just removing the list for version x is that you want to preserve the policy measurement.

This example assumed that the OSV/VMV provided a signed list with an MLE element. If that is not the case, then you will need to sign your own list. However, that allows you to include a PCONF element in the list. Thus you only need two lists.

The same logic holds true for using two PCONF lists (or combined PCONF/MLE lists) for managing BIOS updates or configuration changes.

There is one problem with using signed lists for version control. That is, if an attacker is able to replace your policy file for version $x + 1$ with a copy of your version x policy file, the attacker prevents version $x + 1$ from launching. In addition, if the attacker is able to cause the platform to boot version x instead of $x + 1$, the attacker can exploit any security vulnerabilities that existed in the previous version. This is referred to as a *rollback attack*.

You can prevent a rollback by using the revocation counters. The TPM NV policy data contains eight revocation values (one for each possible list). Each time you sign a list, the tool automatically updates the revocation counter in the list's signature block. Setting the revocation value in the TPM NVRAM to the value of the current list prevents older lists (lists with a lower revocation count) from being used. If malicious code was successful in replacing the policy data file for version $x + 1$ with an older version allowing version x, it would prevent the launch of version $x + 1$ (denial of service), but launching version x would not be permitted. If an attacker is able to get in and manipulate files in your boot directory, then you have bigger problems than a denial-of-service attack. The bottom line is that Intel TXT detects the attack and that the launch failure serves as an alarm.

Using the Simplest Policy

The more complex the launch control policy, the more difficult it is to manage it. Using a policy of ANY is very simple to implement and requires no maintenance. But it also offers the least amount of protection. The most protection comes from using both a PCONF policy and an MLE policy, but there is a tradeoff between maximizing your protection and manageable policies.

So take your time in evaluating what it means if you exclude a particular PCR from the PCONF policy. Is remote attestation in place to take up the slack? Let's take an example.

Excluding PCONF altogether means that the platform is allowed to launch with any platform configuration and any BIOS. This affords the least protection against reset attacks and root kits. However, early remote attestation can prevent any damage that can be done by a corrupted BIOS or a misconfigured platform if it is able to immediately quarantine the platform or prevent it from joining the production network. Such an action should prevent the platform from accessing protected data, and even if it does, the malicious software is not able to communicate that information externally.

Thus, in this case, the need for the PCONF launch policy is negated. The same holds true for the MLE launch policy. Several security management vendors have demonstrated remote attestation products that do quarantine platforms that are out of compliance. Such applications are expected to be released starting late 2013.

Other Tips

Here are some steps that you can take to make managing launch control policies easier.

- For platforms of the same model, use identical platform configurations. This includes using the same add-on devices if those devices contain option ROMs.

- Keep platforms updated with the latest BIOS version. Not only will this help keep platforms consistent, but it assures that you have the latest security patches, ACMs, and microcode patches.

Strategies

So let's factor in your learning curve, availability of tools, and completeness of solutions.

During your evaluation phase, it should be sufficient to start with the default policy established by the OS/VMM. Most likely it is a policy of ANY, or perhaps the OS/VMM vendor provides a signed MLE Only policy. This will allow you to establish trusted pools and evaluate various remote attestation solutions without the burden of setting up and maintaining a launch control policy.

Whether or not this is the right policy going forward depends on a number of factors:

- *Confidence.* Starting out with a policy of ANY and switching to a specific policy at a later time after you have evaluated various policies is a viable choice, even when other factors indicate a more complex policy is desired.

- *Training.* For both you and your staff. Knowing when a policy is likely to fail, the impact of a failed policy, and the recovery actions need to be well known by everyone who maintains the datacenter.

- *Available tools.* Some OS/VMMs provide more complete solutions than others. But they are still on their learning curve and continue to expand their capability with each release. This means that the tools and mechanisms that you need to manage a launch control policy might not be available, or might be very crude and difficult to use.

- *Risk.* More complex policies add the risk that you or your staff could make a configuration change without updating the policy, and thus cause platforms to drop out of the trusted pool or even become temporarily inoperable until the policy is updated.

- *Trusted Pools.* Are they based on remote attestation or on a launch control policy? This is becoming less and less of a problem because remote attestation solutions are becoming more prevalent. Some of the earlier management applications relied solely on a platform's ability to pass a launch control policy as the criteria for it to be added to the pool of trusted servers. This requires a stringent launch control policy. As more and more remote attestations services are introduced, management software will most likely migrate toward using remote attestation services, because they offer more flexibility and capability. At least for managing public clouds. For private clouds, a launch control policy may remain the choice because of its simplicity.

- *Reset protections.* Reset attacks can still occur even with remote attestation. Platforms that use autopromotion for the SBIOS policy rely on the launch control policy to establish if the BIOS is trusted. Thus, a PCONF policy provides greater protection against reset attacks because BIOS trust is established before secrets are placed in memory. This is not an issue for platforms that implement signed BIOS policy because the platform manufacturer provides the known good BIOS measurements.

- *Remote attestation.* By itself, remote attestation does not replace launch control policy. Initially, most remote attestation applications are looking at the dynamic PCRs. This should evolve to cover static PCRs (that is, platform configuration). As applications that rely on remote attestations evolve, they will be able to provide the same protections as the launch control policy, but only if their policy is set to evaluate all of the PCRs that you feel are pertinent. This means that over time, launch control policy could become less important. Before you can dismiss the importance of PCONF policy, you will need to evaluate your management applications for their ability to detect BIOS and configuration changes, as well as mitigation of BIOS corruption.

It is recommended that you start with the default policy and migrate to a more restrictive policy as soon as the proper tools are available. As remote attestation capabilities evolve, you will be able migrate back to the default policy to reduce the burden of policy management.

Starting with an MLE policy and PCONF policy of PCR0 is considered sufficient by many. So this should be your first step toward a more restrictive policy. If you are paranoid (and remember that "only the paranoid survive") you would want to include all the PCRs. Here are some reasons that you might want to exclude them:

- *PCR0.* Always include.

- *PCR1.* Many variations make policy management exceptionally difficult.

- *PCR2* and *PCR3.* You can't control when option ROM code is updated, and thus must avoid such an update from making platforms unavailable.

- *PCR4* and *PCR5.* Any boot source is okay because MLE policy allows only an authorized OS/VMM to perform a measured launch.

- *PCR6.* Not useful because your servers don't support S3 sleep state.

- *PCR7.* Not useful because it is not defined.

- *Any PCR that does not maintain a consistent value from launch to launch.* Excluding that PCR is only a short-term solution. Contact the OEM and ask for a BIOS update that will fix the problem since TCG requirements forbid dynamic values from being extended into PCRs.

- *Any PCR that yields a different value on identical platforms.* Excluding that PCR is only a short-term solution. Contact the OEM and ask for a BIOS update that will fix the problem, because TCG requirements forbid platform identity (or anything that could be used to identify an individual platform) from being extended into PCRs.

Impact of Changing TPM Ownership

There is a difference between *changing* the TPM owner's authorization *value* (TPM password) and *resetting* the TPM password. Changing the TPM password requires knowing the current password and can be performed as many times as necessary without impacting the launch control policy or other TPM resources (other than changing their authorization).

Resetting the TPM password (referred to as *clearing* the TPM) is performed via the BIOS (or the TPM owner) and will invalidate every TPM object that uses owner authorization. This means that the Platform Owner policy in the TPM NVRAM will be deleted. Thus platform owner policy will revert to the platform supplier policy, which is typically ANY or "ANY MLE plus PCR0 matching the signed list provided by the OEM." In any case, it is not the policy that you had established. Your policy data structure still exists, but you will have to re-create the Platform Owner policy in the TPM NVRAM. But that can only be done after taking ownership of the TPM and establishing a new TPM password.

Now you might think that the only reason that you would do that is if you forgot the TPM password (or wanted to sell or otherwise remove the platform from the datacenter). There are other reasons:

- *Switching to a different OS/VMM.* Some OS/VMMs establish exclusive TPM ownership (such as VMware ESXi) and do not allow the TPM password to be known. In order to uninstall such an OS/VMM and install another most likely requires resetting the TPM password. If you don't clear the TPM, you will have to use the original OS/VMM's tools for managing the TPM (if that is even possible). This implies that you will need to maintain a license for the original OS/VMM and that you will have the limitations of those original tools, which are most likely crafted for the needs of the original OS/VMM.

- *Reinstalling the same OS/VMM.* Note that ESXi does not have this problem. If you reinstall it, it detects that it already has exclusive ownership, and thus installs and executes with full Intel TXT capability. Other OS/VMMs might not be as accommodating, and thus require clearing ownership in order to install.

- *In theory, any OS/VMM that takes exclusive ownership of the TPM might be subject to inadvertent corruption of the TPM password.* For example, let's say the TPM password was sealed to the wrong value, or the key that the OS/VMM used to seal the password was inadvertently deleted or corrupted. This would be equivalent to you forgetting the TPM password, and thus require having to clear the TPM and reestablish TPM Ownership.

If for any reason you are required to clear the TPM (or do it accidentally—there is no un-clear), then you will have to reestablish TPM ownership and re-create the Platform Owner policy in the TPM NVRAM.

Decision Matrix

It would be nice if we were able to provide you with a decision matrix that would tell you which launch control policy is best. But that is not possible because it is too difficult to quantify the value of various protections. The best we can do is to provide you with a list of questions for you to consider when determining your launch control policy. The term *OS/VMM default policy* refers to the LCP established by the OS/VMM when it is installed. If OS/VMM does not establish a default policy, then the default would assume that you created a platform owner policy of ANY.

Here is the list of questions for you to answer to help you select the appropriate policy:

- Is remote attestation in place that mitigates the need for a launch control policy? If so, will the OS/VMM default policy be acceptable? Do any of the remote attestation applications rely on launch control policy?

- What is the default OS/VMM policy? Is it ANY or does the OS/VMM provide the list of known good MLE values?

- Do you have the tools to create and manage your own policy? If not, can you use the OS/VMM default policy until you acquire the proper tools?

- How important is it to protect against platform configuration changes? What is the risk that such an attack could occur? Is including PCR1 needed? Sufficient? Or do you need to include PCR4 and PCR5?

- How important is it to protect against unauthorized BIOS modification? What is the risk that such an attack could occur?

- How important is it to protect against an unauthorized OS/VMM performing a measured launch? What is the risk that this could occur?

- How difficult is it to update the policy when there is a BIOS update? An OS/VMM update? A configuration change?

- What is the risk of not updating the policy when there is a BIOS update? An OS/VMM update? A configuration change? Will it result in excessive downtime? What percentage of platforms would be impacted?

- Can you live with the result if any of these risks are realized? Would your company's reputation be tarnished? Would your company survive? Would your job be in jeopardy?

No one said that managing launch control policy was going to be easy, and you will most likely have to make tradeoffs. If you choose anything less than PCONF(PCR0) + MLE, then make sure you can justify your decision.

■ ■ ■

CHAPTER 5

Raising Visibility for Trust: The Role of Attestation

Facts are stubborn things; and whatever may be our wishes, our inclinations, or the dictates of our passions, they cannot alter the state of facts and evidence.

—John Adams

Up to this point, our book has discussed the platform requirements and implementation mechanics for Intel TXT as a function of setting up the server infrastructure. This chapter will now turn to look at the critical capability of how to collect platform trust information for use in more far-reaching operational use models. As the previous chapter mentioned briefly, the capability that makes this happen is *attestation*. Historically and practically, attestation services have been the missing piece of the trusted computing puzzle. This chapter will discuss in more detail what attestation means, how it relates to Intel TXT, the role attestation plays in the Intel TXT use models, and how Intel works with the ecosystem of third-party software and service providers to enable this capability for delivering meaningful and compelling solutions.

Attestation: What It Means

While we will discuss how attestation is a critical component of Intel TXT and its use models, it helps to be reminded that there are actually a number of different attestations at play. They all have some common attributes, because in general, attestations are all about providing some sort of evidence or proof of some platform operation, value, or process.

For a computer security researcher interested in developing trusted computing architectures and technologies, a thorough evaluation and discussion of each definition might be interesting. However, a top-level definition of attestation that matters most to an IT professional who wants to build a more secure datacenter and cloud using technologies such as Intel TXT should suffice. The Trusted Computing Group (TCG) defines attestation as follows:

"The process of vouching for the accuracy of information. External entities can attest to shielded locations, protected capabilities, and Roots of Trust. A platform can attest to its description of platform characteristics that affect the integrity (trustworthiness) of a platform. Both forms of attestation require reliable evidence of the attesting entity."[1]

The evidence and proofs of the platform values are vital in at least two dimensions of attestation (local and remote). And as discussed in Chapter 4, these attestations and proofs are quite complementary. Figure 5-1 shows a simplified process model for attestation in the context of platforms and use models.

---

[1] http://www.trustedcomputinggroup.org/developers/glossary/.

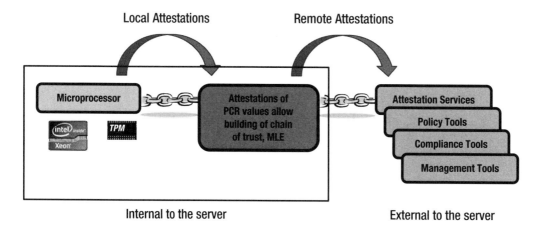

Source: Intel Corporation

Figure 5-1. *Attestations help extend the chain of trust and enable use models beyond the platform*

Local attestations occur within the system. This is the mechanism in which the PCR values are sealed/unsealed by verified modules to establish the chain of trust from the processor-based root of trust. The attested assertions of trust between launch components as described in the launch process in Chapters 2 and 3 are evaluated and used in the context of launch control policy (LCP) through the Intel TXT–enabled boot process. Local attestations occur internally to the server during the crucial initial interactions between ACMs, the TPM, launch code modules, and policy indices. The result of local attestations processes is a platform that is trusted, and capable of UNSEALing secrets from the TPM or determining if it is untrusted.

As Chapter 4 indicated, *remote attestations* provide platform trust values to outside entities. In a nutshell, remote attestation is the method we use to securely expose the results of our trusted launch process and the platform chain of trust to the world—thus providing the "pump" to fuel our operationalized use models for Intel TXT. A server can't assert its own integrity or location. So we need attestation services that will allow us to gather and authenticate platform trust information for use by tools such as virtualization or systems management consoles, security policy tools, and so on. As we will discuss in more detail in subsequent chapters, we can use this trust information to control and report on physical, virtual, and cloud infrastructures and workloads more effectively as it provides greater insights into the state of the platform. Since the local attestations, chain of trust, LCP, and the other platform internals have already been discussed in depth, the rest of this chapter will focus on remote attestation as the enabler to maximize the value for Intel TXT use models.

Attestation Service Components

As you will soon see, attestation provides the fuel that drives Intel TXT use models beyond basic trusted launch of a platform into more scalable, flexible, and operationally valuable assets in the IT manager's security portfolio. Figure 5-2 provides a view of the role that attestation plays in the general abstract system architecture model. It also provides a relatively simple framework to discuss attestation from a component and role perspective. Even looking at it from this general architectural view, the critical central role really becomes clear.

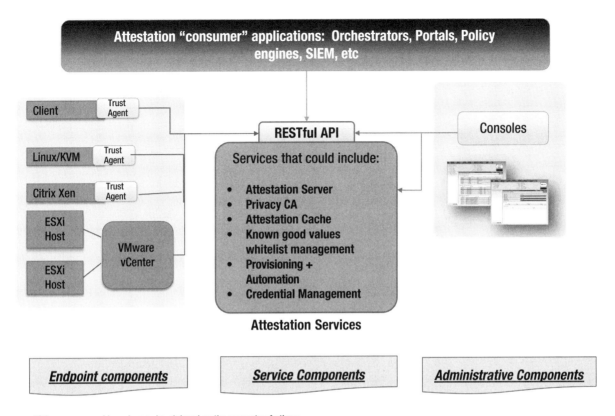

*Other names and brands may be claimed as the property of others

Source: Intel Corporation

Figure 5-2. *An overview of an attestation service conceptual architecture*

From Figure 5-2, we can see that an attestation infrastructure will interface with a number of key components in the IT infrastructure. It touches endpoint devices (which could be traditional clients such as desktops or laptops) as well as server endpoints. The attestation service will communicate to these endpoints through APIs and/or agents on the devices (depending on the architecture) to gather trust status information. The attestation service will communicate with the administrative components such as management consoles to provide status information. And the attestation service will provide attestation results and information to other applications (such as self-service or ordering portals, security policy tools, cloud orchestration applications, etc.) in the infrastructure for the enablement of key use models for trusted computing.

Endpoint, Service, and Administrative Components

It is now time to take a brief review of the roles and architectures of the endpoint components, service components, and administrative components shown at the bottom of Figure 5-2.

Endpoint component capabilities and roles are primarily related to providing the mechanism for *gathering* platform launch status, as well as other potentially useful platform data (such as geotag/asset-tag data, which will be described in Chapter 7) from the TPM, and packaging it for reporting into the attestation server/service. Data from the endpoint will be accessed from the PRCs and NVRAM using TCG-standard TPM Quote mechanics, and packaged using XML schema. In most host operating environments—including Linux and the commonly used related open-source hypervisors such as KVM or Xen, a trust agent will be resident on the host to provide this capability. Note that some hypervisor environments (such as VMware vSphere) provide their own native capabilities for providing platform trust information into the attestation infrastructure. Figure 5-3 shows the process flow for a trust agent capturing platform data and delivering it to the attestation service.

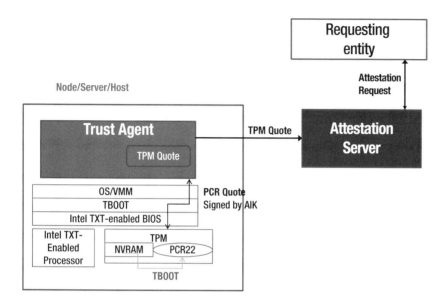

Source: Intel Corporation

Figure 5-3. *Trust agent roles in the attestation architecture*

In this scenario, an external entity (perhaps an administrator at a console or one of the "attestation consumer" applications referenced at the top of Figure 5-2) seeks information about the trustworthiness of the endpoint. The trust agent can work with the platform operating system or hypervisor to issue a TPM Quote from the platform TPMs. (Note that in some cases, the hypervisor or operating system can answer this request natively—without a trust agent). Only a trusted operating system can unseal the hash values within the TPM and issue this response back to the attestation server in the form of a signed TPM Quote. From here, the attestation server can process the quote and provide information back to the requesting entity.

Attestation Service Component Capabilities

The attestation service component capabilities and their role are rather broad. In their simplest form, the primary purpose of the service component is to evaluate and provide platform trust status assertions to other entities for use in trusted pools, compliance, and other key use models. As such, they receive requests for information about a platform, and generate requests to the host to collect the information (hash values) about its trustability, location, and so forth, as described in the previous section. They have facilities to validate the information source (via keys) and compare the reported values (which previously arrived in the SAML assertion of the TPM Quote) against whitelists of known good expected hash values. Of course, this means such services must also possess facilities for building and maintaining whitelists. It must also have a mechanism for packaging responses to the original requests for information about the platform—typically via RESTful APIs. There are often desirable related services such as tools for doing bulk attestations, caching, and so forth, which provide value in terms of enhancing the usability, scalability, and so forth, of an attestation service in a high-volume datacenter or cloud implementation.

It is critical to note that just as authenticity is important for building the initial chain of trust and assertions against the elements of the LCP in local attestation, it is equally crucial that the attested information must be verifiable as authentic to the reporting entity for uses in remote attestation models. Attestation services must provide such facilities for trust to be usable by outside entities. For this reason, you will see security functions such as signatures, certificates, SSL and TLS, SAML, and more, as key capabilities of a core attestation service component. They complement traditional access control mechanisms to help provide tamper resistance, integrity, and authenticity to the evidence generated from the root of trust through the operating and reporting infrastructure in the attestation process. This is especially valuable when one remembers that this attestation infrastructure environment spans not only potentially scores of systems, but virtual physical and even off-premise, third-party cloud platforms. These security capabilities allow IT and security professionals to have confidence in the reporting infrastructure so that these tools can be used for audit, compliance, and forensics work.

Administrative Component Capabilities

The administrative component capabilities shown in the Figure 5-2 overview are fairly basic, and include a portal for the service administrator that provides a way to consolidate, monitor, and display trust status (often using HTML5 tools). This portal provides the administrative front end for the tools used to configure the attestation service, build and manage the whitelist database, and so forth.

Attestation in the Intel TXT Use Models

The preceding sections have described some of the more critical components of attestation services and outlined how these services work to pull launch status and other key information such as geotags from the platform in a secure manner. This capability is foundational and essential to the operation of all the interesting use models for Intel TXT. In short,

- Attestation is needed to securely query a platform to get platform trust and geotag/asset tag information from the platform(s).

- Attestation services provide a manageable whitelist of known good platform hashes—and evaluate trust and location/asset information against this whitelist.

- Attestation services provide trust, location, and information to other enterprise and cloud management and security tools for enforcement (e.g., controlling virtual machine migrations based on defined trust policy) and reporting (e.g., monitoring compliance to policies).

As a result, it can be expected that there would be many attestation activities occurring during the execution and operation of the key trusted launch (determining if one happened on a target platform), trusted pools (providing platform trust attributes for use in enforcing workload migrations), and compliance (providing platform trust attribute data for comparison to expectations and policy) use models. Figure 5-4 shows the use models and general path of attestations for each.

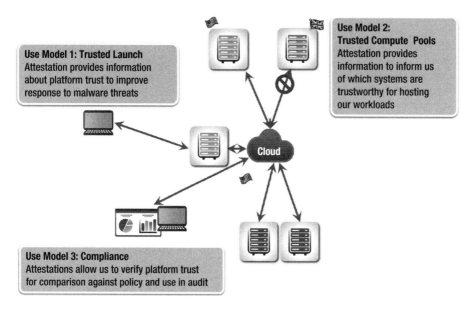

Source: Intel Corporation

Figure 5-4. *Attestations are critical in all Intel TXT use models*

These use models will be described in more detail in Chapter 7, but it is easy to see that attestation really does provide essential services to allow these use models to function. Therefore, it is equally essential that the attestation mechanism has broad accessibility in the infrastructure, as it needs to

- Accept requests for trust status from portals, SIEM, GRC tools, and other entities across an enterprise or between cloud infrastructures.

- Initiate attestation requests from a service to a platform hypervisor, OS, or trust agent (and get host values from TPM) across an array of hosts in, possibly, many dispersed locations. This request may alternately go to the virtualization management layer (for example, vCenter) in VMware implementations.

- Accept and verify TPM Quote responses from the platform against the expected known good list (whitelist).

- Provide trust assertions about the platform via RESTful APIs to the inquiring entities: portals, SIEM, policy tools, GRC, and so forth, for use (as shown in Figure 5-2).

In short, the attestation service provides the mechanism to get trust information securely out of the platform hardware, verify it, and provide it to applications that help IT reduce malware, gain operational control, and meet audit needs.

With all these responsibilities, and all these related touch points, where attestation sits (at least generally) in the architecture is useful to know. Figure 5-5 provides a general architecture perspective to understand where attestation services fit in relation to platforms, cloud infrastructure, management, and security tools.

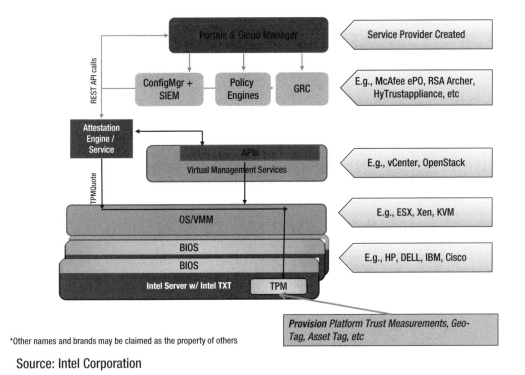

*Other names and brands may be claimed as the property of others

Source: Intel Corporation

Figure 5-5. *Trusted pools attestation conceptual architecture*

Figure 5-5 shows us that attestation services can sit in any number of places—with the core criteria being that it has accessibility to the relevant platforms (the providers of its information) and the dependent consumers of its information (security applications, portals, virtualization management systems, etc.). So in many ways, it can sit anywhere (as long as accessibility can be granted), which means that attestation services could be a cloud service, on-premise appliances, or integrated into any of a number of layers in our stack (though it is shown as a discrete service here). In a similar vein, attestation services could be placed everywhere. Therefore, many layers and applications (both company-owned or provided as a service) can provide their own attestation capabilities, or such capabilities could be federated among a number of applications or service providers. Aspects of how these implementation and integration choices are being made by ISVs and service providers today and how they are likely to evolve will be discussed in greater detail in Chapter 6.

Enabling the Market with Attestation

We mentioned earlier that there was a void in the commercial market for attestation capabilities. In trusted computing components such as TPMs that have shipped by the hundreds of millions over the past few years, saw activation rates that were low and the use models that were in use were relatively contained within the platform—such as SEALing encryption keys for trusted operating systems. There were a few efforts at remote attestation technologies, perhaps the most notable being the OpenPTS project from IBM. But these have been somewhat basic approaches and saw limited implementation at best.

It seems the technology was caught in a classic catch-22: there was limited demand for developers to build solutions because the market had not shown compelling use models. And it was hard to envision compelling use models with no technology to stimulate the solution set. With Intel TXT technology shipping in volume and gaining ecosystem support, and armed with some powerful use models driven by security concerns and the changing dynamics of virtualized and cloud datacenters, the time and opportunity were right for change.

To provide that catalyst for change to the market, Intel undertook two projects to help enable the market to deliver our chosen use models: the OpenAttestation project (often referred to as OAT) and a project code-named Mt. Wilson technology. We'll review each briefly.

OpenAttestation

OpenAttestation is an Intel-maintained open-source project that is a software development kit (SDK) for managing host integrity verification using TCG-defined remote attestation protocols. The project includes code that was developed by the National Information Assurance Research Lab (NIARL) of the US National Security Agency—an agency that has a long history of involvement in developing security and trusted computing technologies. The project is available for use and contributions by all; it is hosted on the GitHub repository, which is commonly used by open-source projects, at `https://github.com/OpenAttestation/OpenAttestation.git`.

Intel expects the primary audience of collaborators, customers, and developers for OpenAttestation to be comprised of cloud service providers and enterprise security and management tools providers. The vendors that have a strong focus on building services and tools based on primarily open-source platforms and technologies, such as Xen or KVM hypervisors and OpenStack, have shown the greatest interest. Generally, this interest is driven by cost (free!), accessibility (GitHub), flexibility (source code, BSD license model), license model, and technology affinity (compatibility with tools and skills).

Of course, it has to do something useful to drive interest, and it does. Some of the key features and services of OAT (as of this writing in 2013) include:

- Supports major Linux-hosted operating systems (including Ubuntu, SUSE, Red Hat Enterprise Linux) and the associated hypervisors (Xen, KVM)

- Java-based privacy certificate authority (Privacy CA) and appraiser for authenticating platform quotes

- Java-based host agent that accesses the platform TPM through the well-established open-source TSS (also known as TrouSerS) trusted computing software stack

- RESTful-based simple Query API with added support for Tomcat two-way SSL/TLS for securing the Query APIs

- Reference CLI Curl scripts for API access

- Basic whitelist service and API, with whitelist management capabilities for building and maintaining whitelists of approved system configuration values

- Reference web portal/GUI implementation to speed interface development

- PCR-based report schema and policy rules with historical PCR data tracking/comparison capabilities

- Flexible access control to the attestation server with hooks for ISVs or service providers to implement custom access control mechanisms

Of course, this list of capabilities will grow over time as Intel and others in the open-source community and elsewhere extend the project to meet new needs. But to help visualize how these capabilities come together, Figure 5-6 provides a graphical overview of the OpenAttestation project components and architecture.

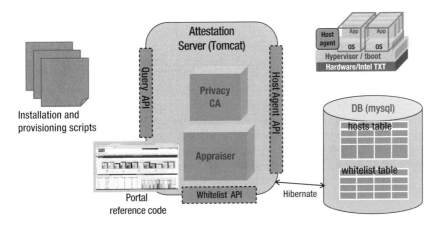

SDK Components

Source: Intel Corporation

Figure 5-6. *OpenAttestation SDK architecture overview*

Hopefully, it is of little surprise that you will note many commonalities in the OAT project components and services and the general attestation architecture shown in Figure 5-2. As it was Intel's intent to enable the solution for the target use models, it indeed covers the endpoint (for example, the host agents), the attestation service (for example, Privacy CA, Query APIs, and whitelist model), and the administrative components (for example, portal and GUI reference code) of the general architecture.

Mt. Wilson

Mt. Wilson technology is the other software project that Intel has applied resources toward in an effort to stimulate the market and assure that solutions to enable use models are commercially available. Structurally, there are many similarities between the two projects, so the authors will spare you yet another visual representation. But it is useful to note that Mt. Wilson is different from OAT in a few key ways:

- Generally more feature rich—including trust agents for platforms not currently supported by OAT

- Developed by Intel (though some open-source components are used)

- Offered in binary (not source code) form

- Offered under an Intel license to a limited number of selected solution providers

Intel chose to undertake the Mt. Wilson program to accelerate the development of solutions. This model allowed Intel to develop more of the components needed to fully enable the use model, and then to share that technology strategically with the third-party ecosystem partners that were most aligned or vital in the marketplace. In short, it was all about solving the technology availability problem for the market. It was Intel's belief that providing a relatively turnkey, binary code base brought significant value for a market that was relatively new to trusted computing. The key allies in using Mt. Wilson are a small number of critical virtualization and security management tools providers, systems integrators and cloud service providers. A key difference is that many of these early partners are more focused on heterogeneous environments or on non-open-source platforms such as Citrix XenServer, VMware vSphere, or others.

The natural next question is usually, "Should I choose Mt. Wilson or OpenAttestation?" The flippant answer that many of us involved in enabling these use models in the industry is, "Who cares?" But the honest answer is that it makes the most sense to let the solution and the software/service provider's needs drive the choice. Ideally, it is best for the ecosystem to select the solution that meets your target market needs or environment, and which suits your business model and skills. Beyond that, it really does not matter much, because the end user or IT administrator customer will likely never know which technology is under the hood of the solution.

That answer might not satisfy all, so we can revert back to our original intent. It is playing out that Mt. Wilson strategically enables key ecosystem partners to use a turnkey package to deeply and more quickly bring solutions to market), whereas OpenAttestation will likely play a broader role over time because it is much more accessible and flexible. But some confusion may be expected, and we have to recognize that software projects and solution needs in a rapidly evolving market can drive the need to change plans quickly. This would be disruptive to the ecosystem. To minimize this issue, Intel has assured that API compatibility between the projects is maintained, and that over time, there will be more common code where there are equivalent services. With these plans, the barrier for an ecosystem provider to change out the core attestation plumbing can be dramatically reduced, and provides them with significant flexibility as their needs change.

How to Get Attestation

Intel's work with the ecosystem, as well as the efforts of others, is resulting in growing success in driving the market for solutions. The best news on this front is that other vendors are also working on attestation technologies now as well, with offerings likely from operating system, cloud, security software, and other types of vendors. Once again, from Intel's perspective, who "owns" or develops the technology is more or less irrelevant—as long as it meets the needs of the solutions and use models. In the end, innovation and customer choice is always the best scenario for customers—and ideally, the technology itself is open and transparent to the IT administrator.

How "transparent" attestation technology becomes will largely be a function of the manner in which it is delivered. Some of the possible models include:

- Dedicated virtual appliances

- Dedicated physical appliances

- Integrated as a function in security application software

- Integrated in cloud management software

- Integrated in virtualization management software

- Offered as a component of a cloud service offering

- Integrated as a "Security as a Service" (also known as SecaaS) offering

In the authors' views, some of these options are less likely than others—and certainly some will come to market faster than others. This last statement we can make with surety from our positions of helping to enable the technology with ecosystem solutions providers. From this vantage point, we can see that some of the first solutions to market will be in the classes of those integrated in security software tools, and cloud and virtualization management. Cloud service offerings that utilize attestation to facilitate trusted pools and compliance use models will also be among the first to market. In each of these cases, the attestation function will largely be "hidden" behind security policy or cloud service creation, management, and enforcement tools.

While this is more conjecture than hard experience on the authors' part, note that other compelling options such as delivery as a component of Security as a Service offerings may indeed ultimately also play a bigger, long-term role in the market. And none of these delivery models is inherently wrong—though in our view, some will do less to lower cost and complexity, and therefore will likely see less broad adoption. Further discussion of where we expect to see attestation services deployed into the software ecosystem is provided in Chapter 6.

CHAPTER 6

■ ■ ■

Trusted Computing: Opportunities in Software

The pessimist sees the difficulty in every opportunity. The optimist sees the opportunity in every difficulty.

—Winston Churchill

Previous chapters have provided some greater insights into the opportunities for implementing, managing, and expanding the value of platform trust as the software and security ecosystem embraces this technology. This chapter will review the critical roles that software and services providers will play to make trust pervasive, scalable, and increasingly useful for businesses of all sizes.

What Does "Enablement" Really Mean?

This book has discussed the enablement of Intel TXT in many different dimensions. It is now a good opportunity to take a look at the impact of trusted computing approaches on the system and software environment and to detail what changes are required to make trust a usable and valuable component of an organization's security arsenal.

Let's start by taking a look at the various layers of enabled use models and how the solutions ecosystem has and will continue to evolve their products to provide higher levels of integrity assurance and trust. Because the use models for trust can be quite extensive and can build from a rudimentary trusted platform to more complex and far-reaching use models, the solution stacks can get somewhat large and perhaps look a bit daunting; we often discuss them in terms of a layered pyramid model, as shown in Figure 6-1.

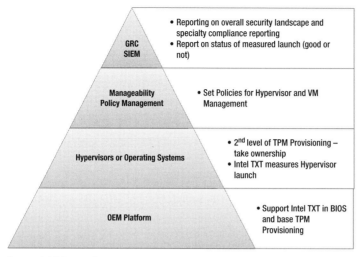

Source: Intel Corporation

Figure 6-1. *The trust use model ecosystem*

As shown in Figure 6-1, there can be quite a bit of enabling required for building full solutions. The functionality for Intel TXT can have impact that spans the hardware and firmware of the server platform, the virtualization layer, or hypervisor (and as noted in previous chapters, bare-metal operating systems in nonvirtualized uses), as well as into the virtualization management and security policy layers, and even into the specialized security incident management and analysis tools (SIEM) and governance, risk, and compliance (GRC) tools domains. In this chapter, we will take a more detailed look at each level in this ecosystem and how they help enable the leading use models. We will also discuss how the various types of ecosystem components are likely to evolve through time.

Don't let this stack intimidate you, though, or lead you to believe that there can be no business value gained until every layer is completely enabled. The simple fact is that not *all* layers are required for *every* solution. What gets implemented will generally depend on the business need and availability of enabled components. Figure 6-2 will help us summarize and map the key requirements for the leading use models with the capabilities and ecosystem needed to realize the use models.

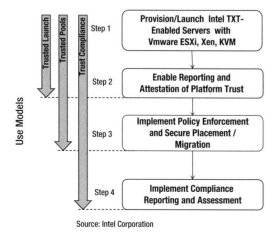

Source: Intel Corporation

Figure 6-2. *Steps and requirements for enabling key trust use models*

As shown, step one is the basic enablement of Intel TXT on a platform—the mechanics of which have been discussed through much of the early chapters of this book. This is a fundamental requirement to get any benefit from Intel TXT, and is core to the enablement of the *trusted launch use model*. The basic function for enabling this capability in the hardware, system BIOS, and operating system or hypervisor is to make sure the critical components of each server get measured during boot.

The next step is to enable attestation (as discussed in Chapter 5) to make the results of the trusted launch process on a given system known by some management entity. Otherwise, only the trusted platform itself would know that it was indeed trusted; so operationally, allowing this information to be collected is a critical complementary function to the trusted launch use model. The next two use models build upon these foundational capabilities.

The third step enables the *trusted pools use model*. The main principle here is that this incrementally enables the centrally collected trust information to be used for decision making by other software in the virtualization and security management tools layer in our model. This will allow new workload control capabilities, which will be discussed in more depth in Chapter 7.

The final step includes extending trust-based integrity reporting and workload controls into the tools of the general SIEM and GRC management tools layers. These can evaluate whether trusted systems and trust-based actions have been compliant with expectations and policies. In short, trusted platforms can become part of enterprise security and risk management suites through proper enablement.

Again, while not all steps or layers must be enabled by every enterprise, there are increased security and operational benefits to be had through having more comprehensive uses and more completely enabled layers. The following sections will provide a bit more detail behind the enablement of each of these layers, which should complement what the reader has already learned in the deployment recommendations from earlier chapters. As with any such structure, it is best to start the discussion at the foundation, so that is where we'll begin.

Platform Enablement: The Basics

Logically—and perhaps obviously—an enabled server has to be a part of any trusted server solution. This book has discussed the inner mechanisms of how the platform can be configured for such use. But how did these mechanisms and tools come to being? And are all created alike? As you will see in further reading, there will be many common capabilities among enabled platforms in terms of protections provided, but some vendors will offer more differentiated solutions and user/administrator experiences that will likely deliver higher value. We'll refer back to our ecosystem pyramid model in Figure 6-1 to guide our discussion as we tease this apart a bit more.

As shown in Figure 6-3, there are two fundamental aspects to creating an Intel TXT–enabled platform. The support for provisioning is discussed here first, and the remote management capabilities required for easier, broad scale deployments are discussed in the next section.

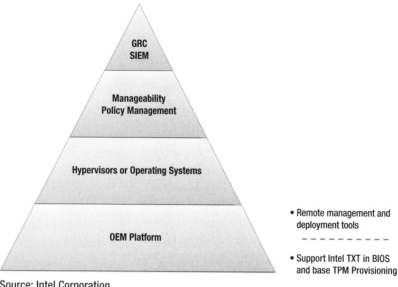

Source: Intel Corporation

Figure 6-3. *OEM platform enablement requirements and opportunities*

These basic capabilities were covered in some depth in our earlier chapters. All systems *must* include these basic functions and features in order to be able to provide the protections and services of Intel TXT. These most basic required elements include:

- A Trusted Platform Module (TPM) on the system, with a firmware mechanism for managing it.

- A BIOS that has been enabled for trusted launch.

As discussed earlier, the TPM plays a critical role for sealing platform secrets and storing trust values, such as our known good measurements, and launch control policy indices to protect them from tampering. Many OEMs have been providing TPMs on a broad selection of their systems or offering them as option kits for some time now. And it is safe to say that they also provide a mechanism in BIOS or firmware to set up and manage the TPM on the local system.

The next requirement is a bit more recent, but also growing more pervasive. This is the requirement to have a BIOS that is enabled for hardware-enforced trust—that can invoke a trusted launch process and allow itself to be measured in the Intel TXT launch process. There is obviously a lot to that task, but in short, the critical components entail the following:

- Integrating Intel-provided authenticated code modules (ACM) that enable and set up the tamper-resistant measurement environment for the BIOS and firmware components.

- Establishing the Firmware Interface Table (FIT) that provides the structure required to put the platform components to be measured in predictable locations.

- Putting structures into the BIOS and menu structures to allow customers to turn on the TPM and Intel TXT.

These new activities are absolutely necessary for the technical enablement of Intel TXT, but in *most* cases will be largely transparent to end users or IT administrators—though some of these elements are reflected in the platform default (PD) policy components discussed in previous chapters. Figure 6-4 provides a screen showing a Dell PowerEdge server providing its easy-to-use options for turning on TPM and Intel TXT functionality on the host platform.

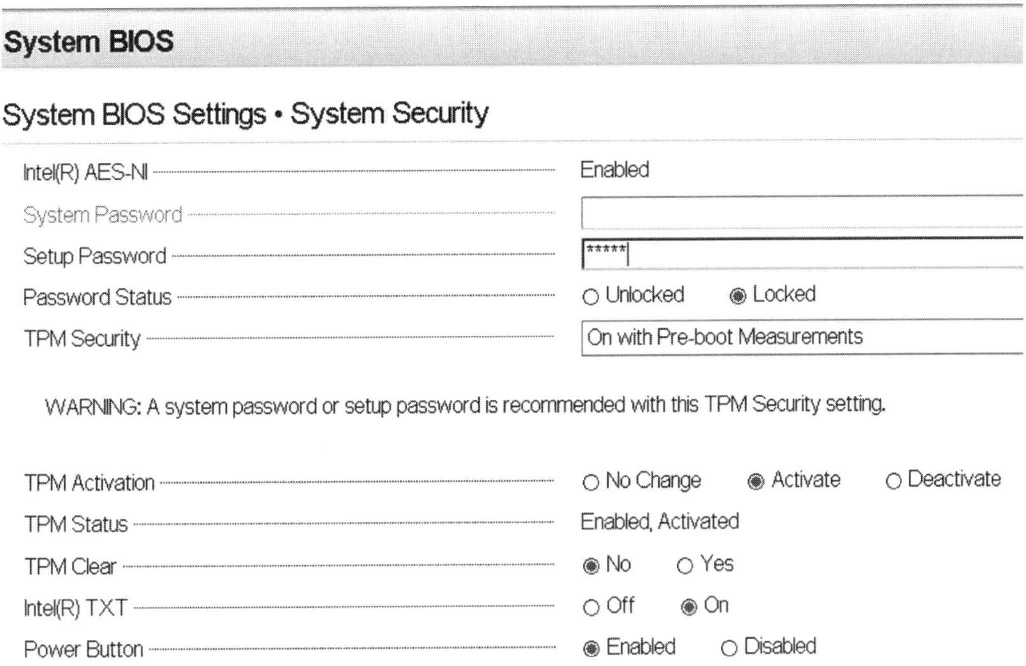

System BIOS

System BIOS Settings • System Security

Intel(R) AES-NI	Enabled
System Password	
Setup Password	*****
Password Status	○ Unlocked ◉ Locked
TPM Security	On with Pre-boot Measurements

WARNING: A system password or setup password is recommended with this TPM Security setting.

TPM Activation	○ No Change ◉ Activate ○ Deactivate
TPM Status	Enabled, Activated
TPM Clear	◉ No ○ Yes
Intel(R) TXT	○ Off ◉ On
Power Button	◉ Enabled ○ Disabled

Figure 6-4. BIOS security setup screen of a Dell PowerEdge 720

This type of menu structure is more or less representative of the IT manager experience with enabled servers—with few exceptions. The authors can only think of a single example in the server industry where an IT administrator will be required to separately install an enabling Intel TXT ACM using a discrete utility provided by the system vendor. An example of this process is the "Gen 8" version of many popular HP ProLiant server models. But note that this implementation model could certainly change in subsequent platform generations or even BIOS releases.

Despite this outlier, we have seen that most of the enabling BIOS structures will have fairly common setups. Some vendors will do more to add value and make it easier and more efficient for their customers to more broadly deploy and manage trusted servers. Much of the variability in this is rooted in how the system vendor designs and implements their BIOS, as well as their tools and utilities for setting up and managing their server platforms. This takes us into the domain of extended platform enablement, as it helps us understand how the underpinnings of trust can be more fully operationalized in a datacenter.

Platform Enablement: Extended

Managing trust is a critical capability. It is also rapidly becoming a fundamental requirement of the modern dynamic datacenter, with perhaps millions of servers on customer sites now capable of implementing Intel TXT. The primary challenge for actually using this capability is the limited awareness of the capability and relative burden of turning it on and making effective use of it. But because the capability is so foundational to some compelling use models, it is reasonable to expect that the ability to implement and manage trust will be an area of continued focus and innovation now that the broad majority of system vendors have incorporated trust technologies into their systems. As much as these vendors have implemented tools to deploy, detect, and manage other system attributes (examples include detecting or predicting component failures, deploying firmware updates, gathering asset information), trust and security capabilities are important aspects of systems to differentiate upon. Vendors will find that this factor is a key to retaining or gaining market share in the years ahead.

Some of the more likely areas where system vendors will enhance their offerings in support of trusted computing include:

- Provisioning

- The update process

- Attestation and attestation services

- Reporting and logging

Each of these steps is vital to making trust usable in the use models described previously or as a complement to existing vendor technologies. And they are also critical to making trust a usable attribute on a datacenter scale. As such, how an OEM facilitates this may become a more significant buying criteria—guiding the selection of one vendor platform vs. another offering a less effective or less easy to use platform. We'll discuss each one in turn.

Provisioning

Provisioning a single system with trust is not a terribly complex operation—though as we've discussed, there is some variation among system vendor implementations. To help solve this small challenge, Intel has published guides for setting up Intel TXT on many of the leading systems from leading OEMS such as HP, Dell, Cisco, IBM, and more. As customer interest grows, we expect that OEMs will build off these early guides to ease customer implementation pain. Even so, beyond that lies a bigger challenge—provisioning dozens, hundreds, or even thousands of systems in a global datacenter operation can take a lot of work. Typically, IT managers use multiple vendor-provided tools such as Dell OpenManage or HP ROM Configuration Utility (HPRCU) to set up and configure batches of servers once they have been "racked and stacked" or otherwise physically set up in the datacenters.

Updates

In a similar vein, IT managers use many of these same tools to manage platform updates—to push out BIOS or other platform firmware updates to targeted platforms in batch mode. Intel and some of the earlier adopters of trusted computing use models have demonstrated that these tools can effectively deploy updates to trusted platforms—using these tools to set up and configure Intel TXT on systems remotely and on multiple systems in a single instance. But here is where the server operational world and the security management world's historical divergence create challenges. Specifically, there is a gap in managing server BIOS and firmware updates and maintaining an updated whitelist of our known good platform configurations. This applies to both the low-level PD and platform owner (PO) policy levels stored in the TPM, but also for consumption in higher-level enterprise security policy tools, which will be discussed later in this chapter. Managing that gap today typically requires manual intervention, new processes, and likely new tools. It makes sense that, over time, traditional server management and update tools will provide the required hooks to automate the update of whitelists and launch control policies when new BIOS and firmware releases are pushed out.

Attestation

Attestation and attestation services are another area where system vendor-provided management tools would be a benefit. Since these tools are widely used to manage a wide array of platform attributes, having an attestation infrastructure that could securely verify platform trust information in the manner described in Chapter 5 would be a logical extension. Attestation capabilities could be used to query the platform at any time, and the results of that attestation effort could be used to generate logs and identify trust events such as a failed trusted launch.

Reporting and Logging

Reporting and logging capability is the final related area where one could likely expect to see significant OEM innovation in the near future. As these tools are often a key resource for IT managers in understanding and reporting on system status and asset management, extending these tools for use in trust and security makes a lot of sense. For example, these tools might be used to maintain the logs of the trusted launch status, or trigger actions in the case of a failed trusted launch in the scenarios from the previous paragraph. Note, however, that this is an area where there are few practical implementations that the authors are aware of to date—even as the number of production and proof-of-concept deployments grows in enterprise and cloud datacenter customers.

It may be the case that security and security management applications may ultimately fill the attestation and reporting roles more naturally and aptly than evolved platform management utilities. One might expect that the balance of how much security management an organization expects of its IT generalists vs. its dedicated IT security professionals may be the ultimate determinant of how quickly (if at all) this role lands in traditional system management tools.

Another consideration is that it is likely not necessary that each of these tools integrates and contains all the functionalities described here. Robust APIs and open, cloud-centric architectures mean that various platform and application layers can share capabilities and data more broadly—using services from elsewhere in the stack to enable the use model at each layer.

Operating System and Hypervisor Enablement

As discussed in earlier chapters, having a bare-metal (i.e., nonvirtualized) operating system or hypervisor enabled for trust is key to all trust use models—one must assure that the controlling software and firmware of the platform has integrity. Figure 6-5 reminds us of the integral position of hypervisors and operating systems in our trusted platforms use model pyramid.

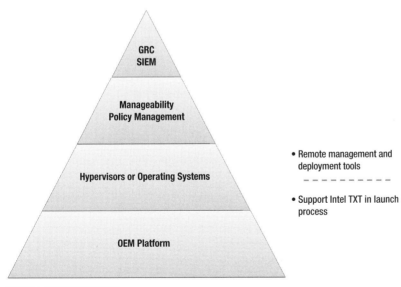

Source: Intel Corporation

Figure 6-5. *Hypervisors and operating systems are critical components of the trusted computing stack*

In the case of Intel TXT, *basic enablement* means that the operating system or hypervisor can invoke the secure launch process. This entails two primary components—the SINIT authenticated code module and a pre-kernel module that can ensure that the right SINIT module is selected and assure the orderly evaluation of the launch components of the software.

Intel has invested years in providing enabling technology for Intel TXT, and has been maintaining the open source "tboot" project as the critical operating system and hypervisor–enabling component for most of that time. Tboot is by far the most widely used mechanism used as a foundation for software vendors to enable their OS or hypervisor. While SINIT modules on server platforms are generally embedded in the platform BIOS and are processor and chipset generation-specific, tboot components provided by Intel are integrated into the operating system or hypervisor by the independent software vendor (ISV) and work across multiple generations of platforms. This makes sense because it allows the most qualified party (in this case, the ISV) to determine which modules are the most essential as the Trusted Compute Base (TCB) of their software, and therefore which modules to include in the measured launch and in which order. These critical component measurements may also be reflected in PO and/or PD policy indices in the platform TPM. Tboot technology is included in multiple open-source operating system/hypervisor environments, from Linux to Xen/KVM, as well as a number of commercial products, such as Red Hat, Citrix XenServer, and more. Other vendors have implemented their own tboot-like functions to enable Intel TXT for trust-enabling their software solutions.

Integrating tboot (or any similar ISV-developed preboot module) is merely the most basic, essential step in enabling—the one that is absolutely foundational to the trusted launch use model. The other core capability that must be provided by the ISV in their operating system or hypervisor is the facility for taking ownership of and managing the TPM. This ownership of the TPM is what will allow the trusted operating environment to be able to SEAL and UNSEAL the TPM-holding platform secrets and to respond to attestation queries—surfacing trust results for use in our critical use models. How an operating system or hypervisor takes ownership of a TPM varies based on the environment—as will the ways someone would use to check his or her platform to determine the TPM ownership status.

Beyond allowing the trusted boot of a platform, much more functionality would be useful for making the trusted computing use models easily deployable in large scale datacenter and distributed cloud environments. In many ways, these added functions address the same types of usability and efficiency challenges we cited in the previous platform enablement discussion. Few of these capabilities are enabled today. While basic enabling of Intel TXT in the operating system and hypervisor is now broadly available, one could expect them to evolve rapidly because initial offerings are maturing in the commercial market and customer demand is growing. Once again, we will consider the key aspects with regard to how the operating system and hypervisors gain enhanced capabilities to support key trusted platforms use models for the following:

- Provisioning

- The update process

- Attestation and attestation services

- Reporting and logging

As discussed, datacenter customers and cloud operators typically deploy systems in bulk and at scale. They use imaging and remote configuration tools to enable consistent software images across scores of systems simultaneously. As we consider trusted platforms and trusted use models, these customer and administrators need tools that will allow them to configure their software environments for trusted computing in large quantities. This is certainly feasible today, with better operational results (for example fewer steps, less scripting, etc.) in some environments than others. Generally speaking, environments that detect and enable platform trust by default (such as VMware vSphere) will make the practice simpler than those that require more customization and configuration of boot files and the like.

A related area that will require far more work is the update and upgrade process. Here again, the main culprit is the immaturity of solutions, resulting in an operational gap—wherein there is a lack of integration in the trust management (for example, maintaining the whitelist of known good versions of the software) and the software image deployment and management process. While minor software updates such as new driver packages and other bug fixes are typically unlikely to impact the TCB, more significant version increments and kernel changes—while infrequent—indeed may necessitate an update to the whitelist and LCP. Today, managing between these disparate worlds requires a similar set of extra steps, tools, and processes, as described in the previous section on platform enablement. If customers are going to get the operational efficiencies of trusted computing use models that they increasingly expect, these gaps must be addressed.

While the operating systems and hypervisors are fairly well established in their ability to establish and manage basic trust on the platform, one could easily envision how native attestation capabilities could be an enhancement to the ability to manage trusted environments. For example, this function could be most useful in the management and update process because it would provide a mechanism for securely querying and verifying platform software versions. Perhaps more practically, merely having attestation services provided through the operating system or hypervisor would establish the functionality almost ubiquitously through many enterprise and cloud customers—and thereby unlocking the most valuable use models. Given the relatively limited technical benefits to adding attestation service natively into the base operating systems and hypervisors, this scenario seems unlikely to the authors, though integration into the management of these layers indeed seems to have both enhanced technical merit and more significant operational value.

Lastly, adding trust-based reporting and logging capabilities would be a natural extension of both the base environment functionality (i.e., software that is responsible for controlling the platform) and the new integral capabilities of this software (i.e., the ability to execute trusted launch). The decision for what trust-related management functions to integrate is likely to be determined as much by the function of how organizations overlay the roles of general IT management relative to those of security management personnel vs. pure technical merit. As a result, even where some number of customers will strongly opt for IT security staff to deal with most platform trust issues with specialized tools, it would still be reasonable to expect at least some incremental capabilities for reporting and logging trust for hypervisors and operating systems for use by IT staff. Given how integral a role trust will play in the hygiene of the overall compute environment, it seems assured that the software will evolve, including some level of reporting and logging infrastructure to reflect trust status and events such as successful or unsuccessful trusted launch; even if this is only to allow the generalist IT administrator to be more effective in maintaining a controlled environment.

Enablement at Management and Policy Layer

Enablement at the management and policy tools layer starts to unlock the higher value of the more advanced and more compelling use models—those of trusted pools and enabling compliance and audit capabilities. It is important to note here that we're talking about a different level of policy and policy tools than the PO and PD policies in the TPM. Here we are talking about specialized security policy tools that allow the enterprise or cloud service providers to define rules, configuration options, and conditions that are approved and appropriate for their business operations and security posture. Quite frankly, the Intel TXT use models are not possible without the management and policy tools that define and control workloads in trusted pools. As one might imagine based on the structure of the pyramid in Figure 6-6, this layer and these tools necessarily follow the base platform and hypervisor and operating system layers.

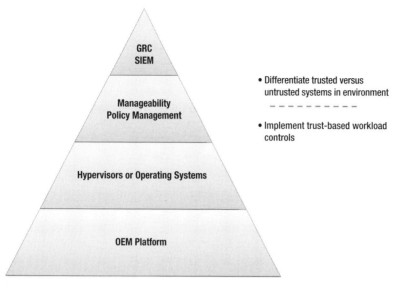

Source: Intel Corporation

Figure 6-6. *Manageability and policy tools provide the functionality to form trusted systems into trusted compute pools*

Even though there are indeed some platform dependencies (after all, one can't build a trusted pool if one has no enabled servers or enabled operating system or hypervisors), there have been fast-moving, visionary, early enablers (such as HyTrust, Virtustream, and Trapezoid Digital Security Services) that have driven the crucial initial implementations and proof points on relatively immature platforms. In an interesting anecdote on risk-taking in this regard, the authors recall working with HyTrust in mid-2009 as they took on the task of working with prerelease Intel® Xeon® 5600 series platforms and VMware ESXi 4.1 hypervisor software to stage the very first trusted pools demonstration for the Intel Developer Forum. Of course, HyTrust, Intel TXT, and the hardware and software ecosystem have come a long way since then, but the foundational premise of trust-based control in the solution remains the same. Figure 6-7 shows a screen the administrator would see when implementing the current Intel TXT-enabled Hytrust solution to gain control over his virtual environment, enforcing trusted pools concepts that we'll discuss in more depth in Chapter 7.

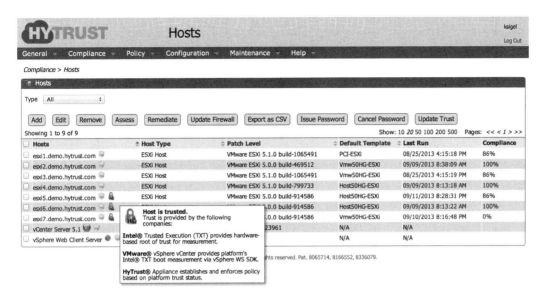

Figure 6-7. *HyTrust Appliance can control VM migrations based on host trust status*

Of course, there have also been those in the ecosystem that have needed to wait for more broad installed bases and customer demand before making enabling investments. But the market is seeing increased awareness and enablement on many fronts as these vendors see the power of these use models to enhance the security of enterprise and cloud environments, and to meet growing mandates for enhanced security.

There are two primary roles of these tools in our use models. These are to

1. Consume the trust information—essentially helping to identify which platforms are trusted and which ones are not.

2. Make use of this information to establish an enhanced security capability through policy definition and enforcement linked to the platform trust.

These two processes form the heart of any trusted compute pools use models. This is where platform trust information is surfaced and used to establish new control boundaries to better manage workloads. These totally new capabilities started captivating customer interest and generated momentum in the marketplace, especially in virtualized and cloud architectures where new controls are desired to replace the lost physical controls of the past.

While the initial implementations are compelling, strong and built with scale in mind due to their focus on cloud and virtualized implementations, it is natural to expect these to evolve as well. In keeping with past practice, let's consider our standard set of value vectors for evolutionary enhancement:

- Provisioning

- The update process

- Attestation and attestation services

- Reporting and logging

Provisioning

It is unlikely that security policy management tools will provide any material enhancements to the trust provisioning process on an individual server or even a set of physical servers. But it is indeed quite likely that the virtualization and cloud management tools can provide better methods to deploy and control platform trust at scale. In fact, this is possibly the essential attribute for the cloud management tools as trusted clouds become a prevalent customer offering. Many cloud vendors are perhaps uniquely positioned to deliver on this enhancement as they typically craft many of their own tools (or even develop their own platform specifications or cloud software) for building and managing their cloud environments. As such, these vendors can implement the tools and technologies needed to solve their scale and operational efficiency challenges in a manner that the broad market may lag.

Updates

This same premise extends nicely to the overall management and update process. While the initial deployment of systems and trust is important, the ongoing management and maintenance is really the more significant hurdle. This is especially true for cloud service providers that require scale and operational efficiency for the profitability of their offerings. Having platform and software updating techniques that are more closely linked to launch and trust policy tools would be a major step in delivering better efficiency. Even the best in class of the early implementers would agree that they have much to do to enhance this aspect of their deployments today—it is still too manual to offer best operational efficiency. Similarly, security policy tools are still likely too loosely linked to the systems and software update processes to provide desired controls or efficiency for such processes. For this reason, most of the security policy and cloud management tools turn to attestation as an abstraction layer.

Attestation

The management and security policy layer is where attestation services, which were discussed in more detail in Chapter 5, have been and will likely continue to be most widely implemented. To date, this has largely been driven by the natural fit between the role of attestation (identifying platform trust status) and the role of the products in this layer—consuming this information and making use of it to control platforms and workloads. There is nothing that leads the authors to believe that this trend will not continue—though this does not preclude that attestation services will be implemented elsewhere in enterprise and cloud deployments. The primary benefit of aligning with native attestation services is that this provides a relatively simple set of REST APIs for obtaining platform trust information on a broad scale.

Reporting and Logging

Reporting and logging functions will also have a similar fundamental value in the management and policy layer as they had in the base operating system and hypervisor layer. It is imperative that the management dashboards have at least some exposure to platform trust status to allow workloads to be managed, and to allow tenants of cloud environments (as an example) to see the status of their environment and to know when or if something unexpected has happened. Certainly, security policy tools must have the capability to report when the policies they define or enforce are broken because the underlying infrastructure is unsuitable (such as becoming untrusted). The initial implementations in the market from HyTrust, Virtustream, and Trapezoid provide such status, logging, and event service natively or through the ability to push this information through APIs, syslog exports, or to other tools (such as GRC and SIEM products) for display or remediation. Figure 6-8 provides an example of how the Trapezoid Trust Control Suite captures and displays platform trust data for IT administrators on a security dashboard.

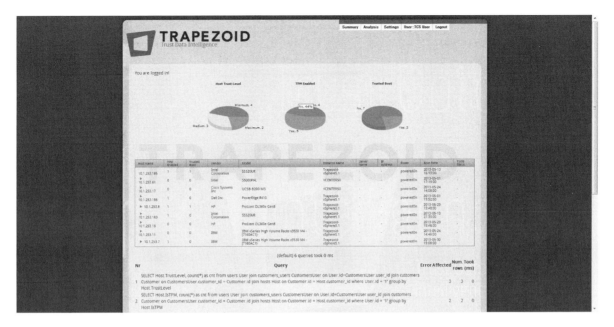

Figure 6-8. *Server trust status can be aggregated, summarized, and graded on a security management dashboard*

In such a view, an IT manager can readily see the trust status of various hosts in their infrastructure, and get access to more details about individual systems to identify where action should be taken.

Enablement at the Security Applications Layer

The security applications layer is comprised of some of the classes of traditional security applications focused on event reporting and managing compliance and risk. The main industry categories for these types of applications are generally SIEM or GRC tools, as shown in Figure 6-9—our now quite familiar ecosystem pyramid.

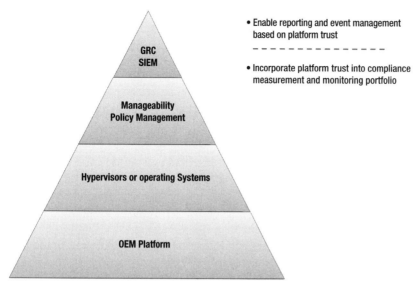

Source: Intel Corporation

Figure 6-9. *Integration with security and risk management tools helps integrate platform trust into security operations and compliance practices*

Because the technologies and use models enabled by Intel TXT involve platform integrity, workload control, and policy enforcement, it makes perfect sense to have such applications aware and enabled to detect, report, and act upon the trust information available from the Intel TXT–enabled platforms.

Intel has been working with market leaders to articulate these use models and how to best reflect them in risk tools and information management tools. One of our earliest examples was a demonstration with RSA in 2010. RSA owns the Archer console, one of the market leaders for eGRC. In this instance, RSA scripted reports that enabled platform trust to be measured and reported into the Archer console. This provided a simple view of platform trust status on a pool of resources, as well as the ability to "drill down" into the specific trust attributes (including hash values of PCRs) of a platform. This last function would be useful in an audit scenario, for example. Intel and RSA have collaborated in subsequent years on further iterations of this rough example in demonstrations hosted at the US Government National Institute for Standards and Technology (NIST).

As such, these tools are critical in enabling the last key use model (shown in Figure 6-2) mapping of technology layers to use models—those focused on enabling compliance to security mandates. These are the tools that business and cloud providers increasingly rely on to monitor and "prove" the protections they define for their workloads and infrastructures.

Similarly, Intel has been working with a number of SIEM vendors so that platform trust events can get logged and reported into the enterprise security management framework. Trapezoid was among the first vendors to demonstrate how to do this using McAfee ePolicy Orchestrator (ePO) as an aggregation layer for platform trust status, then using ePO native interfaces or other APIs and data formats such as Common Event Format (CEF) to export the trust event data (for example, whether a platform trusted launch was successful or unsuccessful) into a number of market-leading SIEM products such as RSA NetWitness, Nitro Security NitroView, TripWire, and more.

Because these products serve such broad security missions, the authors deem it relatively unlikely that many will evolve significant specific capabilities to enhance platform trust use models in the near term—with better provisioning, updating, and attestation capabilities targeting trust. It is entirely natural to believe that these tools that are widely used for monitoring and managing security will become even more trust aware. This means that they should include the requisite APIs to gather (or at least take in) trust status information from platforms. It also stands to reason that they should provide the ability to define reports for measuring compliance with trusted computing requirements for key workloads. The most helpful of these will also include mappings or references to the related "evidence" documentation of—or pointers to—the key standards and mandates that specify the protections and controls required by various institutional, industry, or governmental entities. This closes the compliance loop—stating the protection or control provided and the mandate or requirement that it satisfies.

The various use models for platform trust necessarily require that a complex, multilayered ecosystem would be needed—especially in the early stages of the market. Over time, one could probably predict with confidence that some of these layers and capabilities that are separate or independent today will likely merge or be consolidated in other layers. We have further suggested where some such evolutions of products and offering seem most logical and likely. This aggregation of functionality has a fairly well-established history in the IT marketplace. The only real questions remain in the details:

- Which vendors will lead the charge?

- Over what time periods will it occur?

- Which capabilities or functions will be consolidated into which layers?

- How does the consolidation lower costs, complexity, or otherwise improve the security or operational efficiency of the use models?

The specific answers to these questions are difficult to predict, but the growing emphasis for companies to improve security for their datacenters and in the cloud provides very compelling motivation for players at all layers of the use model stack to look for ways to address risk, cost, complexity, and usability of security solutions for their customers. It opens opportunities for success for new entries into the marketplace. And as mentioned earlier in this chapter, how ecosystems embrace and evolve trusted computing solution models and focus will provide differentiation and influence customers' choice in platforms, software, cloud services, and other solutions. The growing early adoption of the use models outlined in this book will help provide the ecosystem with examples of how they can improve the IT manager and buyer experience for these solutions, and provide much of the catalyst for consolidation.

CHAPTER 7

■ ■ ■

Creating a More Secure Datacenter and Cloud

Every cloud has its silver lining but it is sometimes a little difficult to get it to the mint.

—Don Marquis

This book has discussed the utilities and capabilities enabled by Intel TXT for both datacenter and cloud computing deployment scenarios in numerous places. This chapter will provide more detailed and focused discussion on enabled use models and give examples of available enhanced security for both public and private clouds. It will explain the benefits of integrity, control, and visibility for cloud deployments and discuss various ways that the datacenter and user can take advantage of these attributes to benefit their business.

When Datacenter Meets the Cloud

It is easy and somewhat fashionable to discuss cloud computing models in excited tones as a panacea or a silver bullet that will solve all the challenges and woes of IT. Certainly, there is indeed tremendous interest in cloud computing models, and companies (including Intel) are realizing the benefits of enhanced business agility and cost reduction in their IT environments through adoption of cloud computing technologies and techniques. And analysts continue to recognize and forecast strong growth for cloud products and services. But against this background, we have to recognize that there is still a positively massive investment from businesses of all sizes in what we would think of as "traditional" datacenter IT models. These investments—like mainframe and minicomputer IT models from days of yore—are not going to go away any time soon. A rational perspective can easily see that customers will find ways to adopt new cloud computing models where it makes sense for their business, while continuing to leverage investments in their traditional IT estate, and finding ways to drive new value and efficiency from these investments. In the end, it is natural to expect that many customers will end up implementing some amalgamation of architectures and IT approaches that span traditional, virtualized, and cloud datacenters. As shown in Figure 7-1, while this allows new IT capabilities, it also introduces a number of new security challenges.

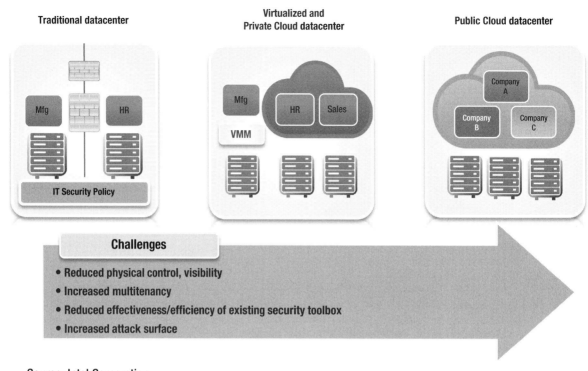

Source: Intel Corporation

Figure 7-1. *IT delivery models evolve to provide numerous options, but create new security challenges*

As you may expect, many of these challenges are driven by the lessening of physical controls—either by moving data beyond a company's four walls and into a public provider's infrastructure or by replacing physical protections such as security appliances with virtual ones. The sharing of infrastructure, in either a public way where the sharing of IT resources with anyone is likely or in a private implementation where the sharing may only be among various business units, may still be problematic. In short, as we look from left to right in the diagram, we see a reduction in control, the reduction in efficiency or effectiveness of traditional security tools, and at least the perception of increased risk of vulnerability.

The challenge of addressing these new security concerns will fall to industry and IT managers alike. In some cases, solutions that migrate from traditional deployments to new models will be the solution of choice. For example, consider how firewalls and a number of other security products that historically have been sold as discrete physical appliances have largely evolved and are now also often available as "virtual appliances" to meet new deployment and use models. But in other cases, entirely new protections and capabilities must be introduced to meet the challenges of new threat vectors, mitigate new risks, and enable appropriate security operation, audit, and compliance models. These new challenges are where technologies such as Intel TXT and its use models really shine.

The Cloud Variants

Before we get more deeply into the security solutions and use models, we should clarify our definition of the cloud. In order to avoid duplicate work and reinvention of the wheel, let's revisit a description that the US government has put in place as a definition of cloud computing attributes as a way of refreshing our perspective and establishing our baseline of understanding.

What is the "cloud"? For simplicity, we can focus on the definition published by the standards-setters at the National Institute of Standards and Technology (NIST) in their Special Publication 800-145 (SP 800-145).[1] The NIST definition establishes a *cloud* as an infrastructure that provides five essential services. These are excerpted as follows:

- *On-demand self-service.* A consumer can unilaterally provision computing capabilities, such as server time and network storage, automatically as needed, without requiring human interaction with each service provider.

- *Broad network access.* Capabilities are available over the network and accessed through standard mechanisms that promote use by heterogeneous thin or thick client platforms (e.g., mobile phones, tablets, laptops, and workstations).

- *Resource pooling.* The provider's computing resources are pooled to serve multiple consumers using a multitenant model, with different physical and virtual resources dynamically assigned and reassigned according to consumer demand. There is a sense of location independence in that the customer generally has no control or knowledge over the exact location of the provided resources but may be able to specify location at a higher level of abstraction (e.g., country, state, or datacenter). Examples of resources include storage, processing, memory, and network bandwidth.

- *Rapid elasticity.* Capabilities can be elastically provisioned and released, in some cases automatically, to scale rapidly outward and inward commensurate with demand. To the consumer, the capabilities available for provisioning often appear to be unlimited and can be appropriated in any quantity at any time.

- *Measured service.* Cloud systems automatically control and optimize resources use by leveraging a metering capability at some level of abstraction appropriate to the type of service (e.g., storage, processing, bandwidth, and active user accounts). Resource usage can be monitored, controlled, and reported, providing transparency for both the provider and consumer of the utilized service.

These descriptions of essential capabilities are quite helpful to guide our understanding of the foundational attributes a cloud must provide. But more discussion is needed still, for we have seen that not all clouds are created equal, with different deployment models and different service models gaining traction in the market. These deployment/delivery models and service models will definitely impact the security capabilities that are needed to give an IT manager or a corporate security manager confidence in deploying workloads beyond a traditional IT model into new virtual or cloud datacenter models.

Cloud Delivery Models

Let's first take a look at the various cloud delivery models. Again, we can repurpose previously published work to establish our baseline for this discussion. In a paper that the authors helped create, Intel IT has published a suitable description of private, public, and hybrid cloud models that we can review here in Table 7-1, with excellent descriptions of the security challenges and considerations included.

---

[1]http://csrc.nist.gov/publications/nistpubs/800-145/SP800-145.pdf.

Table 7-1. *A Brief Overview to Compare Cloud Delivery Models*

Model	Description	Advantages and Disadvantages
Private	• An internal infrastructure that leverages virtualization technology for the sole use of an enterprise behind the firewall • Can be managed by the organization or by a third party • Located on-premises (internal private cloud) or off-premises on shared or dedicated infrastructure (external private cloud)	• Provides the most control over data and platform • Potential for multitenancy of business units to cause compliance and security risk • May lack agility for bursting when additional performance or capacity is required
Public	• Resources dynamically provisioned over the Internet, via web services, or from a third-party provider • Located off-premises, typically on a shared (multitenant) infrastructure • May offer dedicated infrastructure as a response to growing security concerns	• Potential for greater cost savings if infrastructure owned and managed by public provider • Loss of control of data and platform • Potential for multitenancy with other organizations to cause security risk • Third-party security controls possibly not transparent (and may cause unknown risks)

Hybrid	• A combination of private and public cloud services
	• Organizations that often maintain mission-critical services privately with the ability to cloud burst for additional capacity or add selective cloud services for specific purposes
	• Located on-premises and off-premises depending on the architecture and specific services
		• Often a compromise:
		  • Retention of physical control over the most mission-critical data, but relinquishing that control when additional capacity or scale is required during peak or seasonal periods
		  • May involve retention of physical control for mission-critical data at all times while taking advantage of public cloud provider services for less sensitive areas
		• Potential for complexity to cause unknown vulnerabilities (and unknown risks)

■ **Note** Adapted from the Intel IT Center *Planning Guide for Cloud Security*

As you can see, a sizable portion of the challenges are the result of the loss of physical control over workloads and data that occurs as one moves from a private cloud model to a public or hybrid model. This is likely not surprising given that there were similar concerns from customers as they looked at the cloud and virtualization relative to their traditional datacenters. In that scenario, they lost security capabilities and efficiencies through approaches such as physical isolation and discrete appliances as they moved to virtual shared infrastructures. Public and hybrid clouds exacerbate such concerns as they add the element of customers giving up physical control and possession of the workloads and data, as well. So they will need new protections to compensate for this, as well as new ways to view, control, and monitor how their data and workloads are being protected. And in the cases of data and workloads subject to compliance mandates and regulation, they need tools to help audit and prove these protections are in place.

It must be noted that there are few such regulations specifically calling for platform trust today, for it would be impractical to legislate controls and protections that are not widely available or implemented. Part of the motivation for this book is to help stimulate such deployment. But there are a number of regulations and controls that platform trust generally helps address today. These include sources such as the Federal Risk and Authorization Management Program (FedRAMP), the Cloud Security Alliance (CSA) Cloud Controls Matrix, NIST BIOS protections guidelines, and more. And as the maturity, awareness, and ubiquity of trusted platform solutions grows, it is natural to expect that more specific mandates for such protections will get incorporated into policies and regulations for cyber security in various deployment models.

To complete the cloud discussion, we still need to look at the various cloud service models to assess the security implications to determine what new protections and capabilities these might require. Once again, the authors would like to repurpose established definitions created by Intel IT to simplify the discussion, as these match terms often used in the industry. The primary cloud service models discussed in the market and by analysts are shown in Figure 7-2 and include Platform as a Service (often abbreviated as PaaS), Software as a Service (SaaS), and Infrastructure as a Service (IaaS).

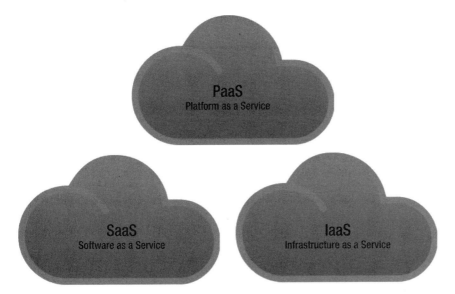

Source: Intel Corporation, Excerpted from IT@Intel Brief "*Intel Cloud Computing Taxonomy and Ecosystem Analysis*"

Figure 7-2. *Summary of the primary models of cloud services*

The Intel IT paper defines these service models as follows:

- SaaS is a model of software deployment in which an end user or enterprise subscribes to software on demand. SaaS applications are built with shared back-end services that enable multiple customers or users to access a shared data model.

- PaaS is the delivery of a cloud computing platform for developers. It facilitates development and deployment of applications without the cost and complexity of buying and managing the underlying hardware and software layers. PaaS provides all the facilities required to support the complete life cycle of building and delivering web applications and cloud services over the Internet.

- IaaS is the delivery of technology infrastructure—such as network, storage, and compute—as a service, typically through virtualization. Users subscribe to this virtual infrastructure on demand as opposed to purchasing servers, software, datacenter space, or network equipment. Billing is typically based on the resources consumed.

Once again we now have a set of service models that give customers significant options for the types of infrastructure they consume—and what services they are receiving from the cloud service provider. These models also pose different levels of control—in terms of who is responsible for what. For example, in a SaaS model, a SaaS provider such as Salesforce.com is responsible for much of the application infrastructure as well as the physical hosting infrastructure. The SaaS customer more or less is only responsible for the data and controlling access appropriately in this model. Alternately, an IaaS provider such as Amazon EC2 or Rackspace will typically only provide availability of basic compute, network, and storage resources on an allocated or "pay as you go" model—with no application or operating environment provided. Of course, these lines may blur over time, and providers could indeed grow from a pure IaaS play to offer applications or more complete platform offerings, but that would basically only change their label—as long as they also evolve their security controls capability as well. For as you can see, these deployment models expose real security implications for customers as they need to consider what they are putting into the cloud infrastructure and how they can protect it and meet any policy compliance requirements. Intel TXT and its use models offer an opportunity to help provide new visibility and controls into this chasm as well as to help provide bridges and common capabilities across traditional physical datacenters and the emerging virtual and cloud IT infrastructures. And in time will likely also be useful in providing a common control capability that can be used across cloud providers, which will be useful for those companies that turn to multiple cloud providers for various services.

Intel TXT Use Models and the Cloud(s)

This book has discussed the enablement of Intel TXT in multiple chapters and in many different dimensions by this point. It is now a good opportunity to take a closer look at the impact of trusted computing use models to make sure the reader has a similarly strong understanding of how this technology can improve the security posture of their IT environments (physical, virtual, or cloud). Figure 7-3 provides a snapshot of the three leading use models for platform trust based on Intel TXT. Each use will be explained in more detail further in the chapter, but the basic premise is that the trusted launch process provides value in assuring platform integrity—lowering the threats and costs of certain classes of stealthy malware. The trusted pools use model extends that value by using the platform integrity enforced and reported by Intel TXT via attestation to be used to control workloads in the cloud. Lastly, the compliance use model extends this value yet again by providing an auditable infrastructure for verifying that the platform and workload controls are in place.

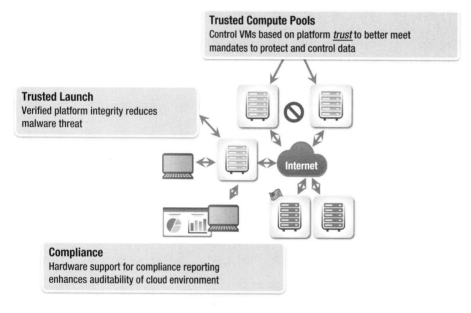

Source: Intel Corporation

Figure 7-3. *Summary of the primary use models of Intel TXT–enabled servers*

The Trusted Launch Model

The initial and foundational use model for Intel TXT is one that has been outlined in much of the first four chapters of this book; this is the ability to execute a trusted launch on a server. This fundamental capability to establish the integrity of a server has benefits for traditional datacenters as well as virtualized and cloud based servers. After all, everyone benefits from a more malware-free environment and Intel TXT, running on servers built with Intel® Xeon® processors, works with enabled software to help protect systems from BIOS and firmware attacks, malicious rootkit installations, and other malware attacks, while providing hardware-based verification that can be used for meeting compliance requirements. As detailed elsewhere in this book, the solution works by providing a processor-based, tamper-resistant environment that compares firmware, BIOS, and operating system or hypervisor code to known good configurations to establish a measured, trusted environment prior to launch. If trust is not verified, Intel TXT identifies that the code has been compromised, which lets you protect the system and remediate the problem. Figure 7-4 summarizes the high-level steps in the trusted launch process.

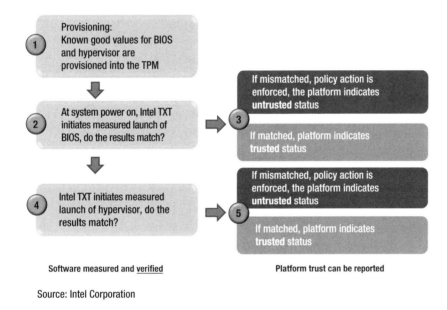

Figure 7-4. *Steps of the trusted launch use model for Intel TXT–enabled servers*

As shown, the process starts with the establishment of the "known good" values of the approved BIOS and hypervisors that should run on the platform. These are provisioned to the TPM module, as discussed in earlier chapters of this book. At power on, the BIOS values are measured. If the BIOS measurement values are the same as the known good values stored in the TPM, then the hypervisor can be measured. But if the BIOS value results don't match, the platform will be proven untrusted. Similarly, if the measured hypervisor values match the known good values in the TPM, then the platform will be proven trusted and secrets can be unsealed, and so forth. If the hypervisor values do not match, then once again the platform will be proven untrusted. If a platform was expected to be trusted but failed these trust checks, then IT can be notified and remediation actions can begin, and other tools using the platforms can be aware and take appropriate measures.

By starting with a root of trust and measured launch environment (MLE), Intel TXT offers you better protection from malware and important visibility into the integrity of your system than would be available from a platform that cannot provide a root of trust or which is only protected by software. There is growing recognition in the industry press, among the analyst community, and from computer security specialists such as the NIST (which has published Special Publications such as SP 800-147B *BIOS Protection Guidelines for Servers*)[2] that discuss the threats from low-level platform attacks and how mitigations such as a hardware root of trust can help address these threats.

As discussed in the opening chapters of this book, and as we focused on in more detail in Chapter 6, this use model requires the most basic but most limited ecosystem enablement to activate. In summary, trusted launch enablement has impact in server hardware and BIOS, and in a suitable operating system or hypervisor that is capable of a measured launch.

Trusted Compute Pools: Driving the Market

The next use model has added benefits for customers that are deploying virtual and cloud IT architectures—as it allows the reintroduction of physical control capabilities into these increasingly shared and abstracted compute models. Trusted compute pools (TCP) are physical or logical groupings of computing platforms in a datacenter that have demonstrated integrity in key controlling components (such as BIOS and hypervisor) in the launch process. Intel TXT provides a hardware-based mechanism for verifying and reporting on platform trust as a foundation for the creation of trusted pools.

Platform trust status is attested to at launch (in the process outlined in Chapter 5) and if the launch was trusted, that platform is added to the trusted pool. Within this pool, systems and workloads can be tagged with security policies, and the access and execution of applications and workloads are monitored, controlled, and possibly audited. The most obvious premise is that highly confidential and sensitive applications and workloads would be constrained by policy to only run on systems that have proven to be trusted. Figure 7-5 outlines the basic steps to show how trusted pools could be used to enable workload controls in a virtual or cloud deployment.

---

[2]http://csrc.nist.gov/publications/drafts/800-147b/draft-sp800-147b_july2012.pdf.

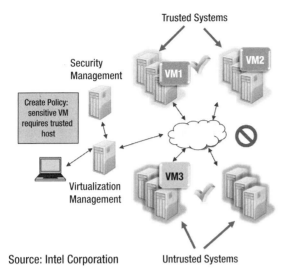

Source: Intel Corporation

Figure 7-5. *Core components of the trusted pools use model for Intel TXT–enabled servers*

The basic steps for enabling a trusted pool start with having some mix of trusted and untrusted systems, as shown in Figure 7-5. From there, it is a matter of five general steps to create the operational trusted pools:

1. Virtualization management software can identify and report platforms that demonstrate integrity via Intel TXT using attestation mechanisms.

2. Security management software allows identification of sensitive workloads, in this case creating "labels" for the sensitive workloads, depicted in this figure as different shaded VMs.

3. Security management software can read platform trust status for the various available hosts from the virtualization management software—providing insight into the security capabilities or attributes of the hosts.

4. Security management software allows linkage of platform capability to workload classification via policy. In this example, a policy is created that specifies that sensitive VMs depicted at the top right in the figure can only run on trusted hosts.

5. Security management software policy can control VMs based on platform trust to better protect data, blocking deployments or migrations of these sensitive workloads into untrusted systems while allowing deployment or migrations among trusted hosts.

The trusted pools use model has gained perhaps even greater market interest than the basic platform trusted launch use model. This is perhaps not surprising since the need for new controls to address the security challenges of the new virtual and cloud use models is so great. Leading companies and agencies in governments, financial services, healthcare, and other industries, as well as cloud service providers that focus on these vertical market segments, have taken the lead and have done some of the initial deployments that serve as case studies for their peers to follow. Companies such as Florida Crystals, DuPont, and the Taiwan Stock Exchange have published testimonials outlining how their initial implementations have delivered security benefits and enhanced their confidence in cloud deployment models in their businesses. This list of success stories is poised to grow as the ecosystem of enabled technologies expands. It will also be fueled by Intel CloudBuilder reference architectures and OEM and ISV solution deployment guides, as well as books such as this one, to help customers understand how to implement solutions in their compute estate. Of course, as these controls get proven out by these ongoing deployments, it is easy to envision industry and regulatory codification of these mechanisms into data and platform protection guidelines and mandates.

To refresh and summarize: the trusted pools use model will indeed require a more significant set of enabled products and technologies to allow this robust, policy-driven security capability across physical, virtual, and cloud infrastructures. As outlined in Chapter 6, it will require the same platform (hardware, BIOS, and operating environment) enabling as the trusted launch use model. It has additional enabling implications for management and policy definitions and enforcement capabilities in terms of comprehending platform trust and integrity values, and implementing workload and data controls based on this information.

Extended Trusted Pools: Asset Tags and Geotags

While the market has rapidly grasped the concept of trusted pools as a new control mechanism and boundary model for enabling more security for their virtual and cloud IT architectures, some leading ISVs and end-user customers are taking an even more visionary approach and working with Intel on a natural extension for this model. The basic thinking behind this is that if Intel TXT-enabled platforms can provide visibility and new control and reporting mechanisms in the cloud, based on platform trust and attestation capabilities, could a trusted platform also store and report additional information that would provide further valuable control capabilities? As it turns out, the answer is "yes."

There are two general types of "new" control capabilities that customers desire. The first one is some type of geographic descriptor (what we often refer to as a *geotag*). After all, one of the natural concerns to address for the cloud is to be able to determine the answer to "Where is my stuff?" In a cloud without boundaries, this is impossible to answer. In a cloud that can be marked with trust and geographic description information, answers to this question can be made trivial—providing new confidence to customers. Given the large and growing number of regulations that stipulate location controls—particularly for privacy-related workloads and government data, this adds a significant breakthrough value. Now, workloads and this kind of data control that fall under the auspices of such regulation are now possibly open to cloud deployments.

The other related type of control that customers have asked for is what we refer to as an *asset tag*. An asset tag is essentially just another set of descriptors that a customer may want to provision into their infrastructure to provide boundaries for controlling workloads and data. One could see an example where a cloud service provider may want to tag some of its compute infrastructure as belonging to different geographic availability zones or as systems with higher performance characteristics or even as dedicated to certain customers or customer types. These scenarios could provide solutions for customers paying for premium SLAs, or if they are servicing competitive customers that want assurances that their competition does not share a common infrastructure with their sensitive workloads. Similarly, by implementing asset tags, such as organization name or department, a customer could implement boundaries in a private cloud deployment. This could allow the IT or security organizations to keep data from different business units or organizational entities from commingling on common infrastructures. For example, this could be useful if a company wanted to make sure that financial, transaction processing, or human resources or other data did not become inadvertently exposed to other systems and data sources—but still wish to gain the benefits of virtualization and cloud computing models.

These tags are merely small text strings that can be populated or provisioned into the TPM. As such, the same Intel TXT–related trust infrastructure (for example, TPM and attestation services) that can store and report trust values can incrementally be provisioned with these additional geotag or asset tag descriptors. This would provide two benefits:

- Assurances that the tag descriptor values are coming from a trusted identifiable entity.

- The opportunity to leverage common attestation tools or services to gather, verify, and provide both trust and other descriptor values to the management, policy, and control infrastructure for use in deploying and securing workloads across infrastructures.

These benefits offer both security (and after all, if you can't trust the platform, you can't trust it to tell you where it was, what uses are appropriate, or anything else about it) and operational efficiency benefits that would be hard to replicate in other ways.

Figure 7-6 provides an example illustrating how platform trust and geolocation information can enable servers to provide enhanced, more granular control capabilities for critical or sensitive workloads. Of course, the greatest benefit comes when these are fully operational and the controls are driven by policy across the physical, virtual, and cloud environments.

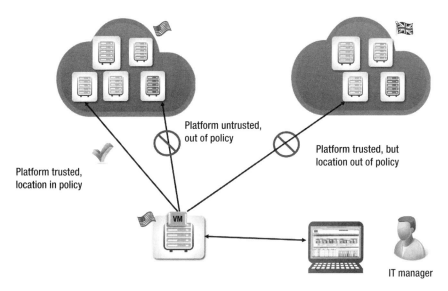

Platform untrusted,
out of policy

Platform trusted, but
location out of policy

Platform trusted,
location in policy

VM

IT manager

Source: Intel Corporation

Figure 7-6. *Extending the trusted pools use model with geolocation and other asset descriptors provides additional visibility, control, and compliance capabilities*

In this example, an IT manager can access platform trust status and an additional descriptor of a geotag from a number of platforms. Behind the scenes, Intel TXT provides the trusted state and geotag descriptor via attestation capability, while untrusted systems may be from platforms that are not enabled with Intel TXT, and on these systems trust cannot be verified. In any case, the IT manager can create a policy that dictates that the workload is sensitive and must reside on both

- A trusted host (to better protect it from malware)

- A host located in the United States (perhaps due to company policy or where the data may be subject to Federal Information Security Management Act (FISMA) boundary control regulations, for example). Note that many other governments have similar regulations for assuring data stays within their governance domains.

Intel TXT and attestation capabilities provide the required insight into the platform to allow actionable data control policies in multiple dimensions—trust and location—using a common set of technologies.

So what does one really get from this extension of trusted pools use models with asset tags or geotags? Let's summarize and consider potential examples from the preceding scenario. The benefits include:

- *Increased visibility*. IT managers gain a hardware-based mechanism to verify platform integrity (trust) status and to store/report other asset descriptors, such as location, for use in their security controls portfolio.

  Example: IT infrastructure can attest to know which platforms have proven integrity, and which have not. IT can get assurances from trusted platforms regarding where cloud-based systems are located or other customer or cloud service provider–defined attributes are in order to implement data/workload controls.

- *Enhanced control.* IT managers can use platform integrity (trust) status and asset descriptor information to control virtual workloads.

  Example: Platform trust and other asset information can be used to implement policies that restrict sensitive workloads. It can be used to enforce policies to control migration or bursting to trusted systems and systems in specific geographical locations, as shown in the preceding example and illustration.

- *Automated compliance support.* IT or information security managers can attest that platform integrity (trust) status and asset descriptor information meet policy and verify that controls are in place and operational.

  Example: A governance, risk, and compliance (GRC) software suite can verify that platforms are trusted as expected and that workload controls for trust and location are established and enforced. In the preceding example, these GRC tools would gather platform trust attestations, as well as record that workloads are being placed in accordance with geographic restrictions and are issuing warnings when these policies were not adhered to.

From a governmental perspective, once again, the US Department of Commerce's NIST organization has been at the forefront of defining desirable and useful new controls to enable the cloud to be a more suitable environment for government workloads. NIST collaborated with Intel, RSA, and others to build a model that expanded on the trusted pools concept to implement location descriptor–based controls on top of trust-based controls to manage and measure compliance for workloads and data in the cloud. The resulting recommendation from this proof-of-concept model, NIST Interagency Report 7904 *Trusted Geolocation in the Cloud: Proof of Concept Implementation*,[3] was published as a draft in January 2013. From there it was presented to a broad set of governmental agencies and opened to comments from other industry participants. Interest and feedback has been very positive and will likely lead to continued enhancement and refinement of the model.

This use model is slightly less mature than the trusted pools use models. The tools for provisioning these tags or descriptors in the Intel TXT-enabled platforms are still nascent, and customers and service providers will need to define the processes and taxonomies for managing the tag values that represent the boundaries for control. But the strong market interest and lure of attracting regulated workloads to the cloud promises to drive rapid maturation of solutions in this space. In a twist that might surprise some, the platform and operating system/hypervisor tools will likely lag behind the ability of the management and policy tools to implement these extended control capabilities. This is, of course, contrary to the maturation model we have seen with the initial use models for Intel TXT.

Compliance: Changing the Landscape

We have seen that with new threats and new IT architectures, new controls for data, workload, and infrastructure are needed. And it is only natural that new mechanisms to enforce security policy and audit compliance to these security requirements are also required. As discussed previously, Intel TXT provides new enforcement mechanisms to support enhanced security for the datacenter, virtualized server environments, and the cloud. The hardware-based system integrity enforcement capabilities of an Intel TXT platform also provide a reporting mechanism to provide visibility into system status. This provides a method to implement and monitor controls and reporting tools across cloud and physical infrastructures via attestation. These Intel TXT, TPM, and attestation features assist in the verification and audit procedures, locally and remotely, to facilitate compliance automation. This is a critical capability for remedying what were previously considered insecure IT infrastructures to make them suitable for use with more critical and sensitive workloads.

Compliance is a topic that we have touched upon briefly in previous chapters. In an increasing number of situations, it is not enough to provide protection for a type of data or component of infrastructure. It is often equally important to be able to monitor and prove that the protection is in place. Traditionally, this is often done with

---

[3]http://csrc.nist.gov/publications/drafts/ir7904/draft_nistir_7904.pdf.

security monitoring, logging, and compliance tools. It is also often done with a labor- and time-intensive audit process, one that gets much worse in virtual and public cloud implementations where an audit spans beyond physical, on-premise situations.

Platform trust is in an interesting position because it is only now starting to gain traction as a mandated or recommended protection (after all, it would be counterproductive to mandate a protection that was not readily available in the marketplace). But as these mandates develop and spread—such as the mapping of the trust and geolocation controls from the NIST IR 7904 recommendation, to the FedRAMP controls recommended for US government cloud purchases. For other regulation, such as the Health Insurance Portability Accountability Act (HIPAA) and International Organization for Standardization (ISO) 27000 series security control standards, trust use models will be ready to enable compliance.

Intel has long been collaborating with the ecosystem to implement controls based on Intel TXT and to show how they can be viewed, monitored, and reported remotely using common security compliance tools. In fact, in early 2010, Intel and RSA teamed with VMware to demonstrate compliance in the cloud, with a public demonstration and a published solution brief titled *Infrastructure Security: Getting to the Bottom of Compliance in the Cloud*[4] that addressed the need for controls and reporting on controls for cloud implementations. The screenshot in Figure 7-7 provides an excellent example. In the demonstration that this represents, the concept was to enact policies for restricting workloads subject to NIST SP800-53 (often referred to as FISMA) regulations to trusted hosts and related boundary controls for US locations. The RSA Archer GRC console was able to test and report on the trust status of the hosts in the demonstration configuration. The console provided a top-level compliance report, as well as a mechanism to get additional information that would be useful for audit purposes.

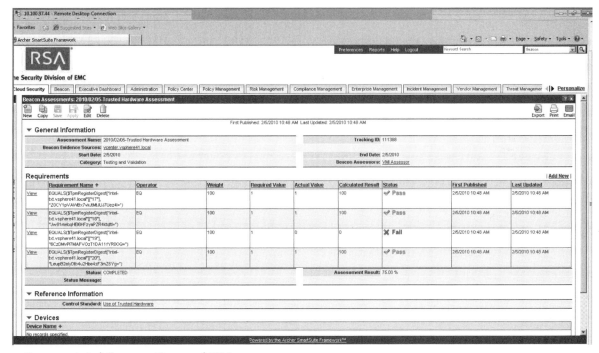

Source: Intel Corporation and RSA

Figure 7-7. *Screenshot of compliance dashboard reporting on platform trust*

---

[4]http://www.rsa.com/innovation/docs/CCOM_BRF_0310.pdf.

It has been interesting for the authors to observe how the market has responded to the use models for Intel TXT through time as we work to enable the industry and evangelize solutions for the market. Perhaps we have been too technology- or threat-focused and not as operationally aware, but the response to compliance use models has been surprisingly strong. Whereas the incremental technology is somewhat minor, the value customers perceive from compliance is quite large. Once again, this is likely due to the large void in controls created by virtualization and cloud architectures, as well as the added audit challenges and resultant cost and time burdens these create.

As trust-enabled solutions get enabled by the security ISV ecosystem, deployed in IT, and supported in the market by leading cloud service providers, compliance use models will be as important a factor in their purchase and deployment justification as the controls themselves. In some cases, it will be even more so as compliance changes the buying equation in an interesting way. Let us explain.

Typically, selling security is about managing risk—real and perceived. Many protections and controls are justified based on the premise that it will reduce or eliminate threats and risk. This is an equation that is often highly subjective. What one customer believes is a real threat or risk, another customer might find irrelevant or a corner case. Mandates that specify or recommend specific or classes of controls start to remove some of this subjective judgment. And in many cases, these governmental, industry, or corporate mandates add an incremental onus on the ability to verify that the controls are in place. Tools that facilitate this across IT architecture types are increasingly essential to making security operationally efficient.

■ ■ ■

CHAPTER 8

The Future of Trusted Computing

The best thing about the future is that it comes one day at a time.

—Abraham Lincoln

This chapter reviews the critical capabilities of a trusted platform and reinforces the benefits of solutions based on Intel® Trusted Execution Technology (Intel® TXT). It discusses the key considerations for implementations and the recommended uses for customers seeking to get started. This chapter also provides a vision of what is to come—explaining why building the infrastructure now will make it easier and quicker to adopt next-generation, trust-based solutions. These new solutions can enhance IT architectures to meet evolving business needs by providing even greater control and visibility into their increasingly virtualized workloads and providing solutions to enable the transition from traditional static datacenter models to embrace new dynamic cloud infrastructures.

Trust Is a Foundation

Increasingly, security is not an option. It is a critical consideration for nearly every business decision: it informs or influences the products that IT buys, the architectures they employ, and the services they subscribe to. With the constantly changing IT architectures, regulatory environment, and potential threats, customers need more tools to provide security in virtualized and cloud environments. The traditional IT security toolbox is just not up to the task to handle all of these changes—with the following being some of the biggest challenges:

- Tools cannot provide coverage to protect assets.

- Tools are no longer architecturally efficient in how they provide protection.

It is already painfully clear that the gap between security capabilities and solutions is a drag on customer adoption of new architectures and use models for the cloud. One can read about it in the trade press on essentially a weekly basis or in discussions with customers or peers, but it is readily evident in nearly every survey that security is a challenge in a global sense.

As shown in Figure 8-1, customers need more protection and controls to make the cloud a viable model for all kinds of workloads. They need protection against emerging threats such as rootkits. Historically, many have viewed these threats as "someone else's problem" or one that is purely hypothetical. Neither is really true. These classes of stealthy, low-level threats are real and occurring "in the wild." The recent example of the "Mebromi" BIOS rootkit (Giuliani 2011) was an eye-opener for many. This attack was specifically engineered to target system BIOS code developed by Award for a number of Chinese computer systems, and capable of detecting the presence of several common local antivirus software packages in order to thwart them. Similarly, the discussions driven by Invisible Things Lab with their "Blue Pill" Hypervisor rootkit concept (Rutkowska/Tereshkin 2006) dramatically raised the visibility into security concerns with hypervisor software models. Most were unaware that such esoteric platform components could be attacked and that an attack could be executed in a commercial environment. Unfortunately, as is often the case, it takes a commercial exploit to change the mindset and drive people to take action. And there

119

are many more IT managers and security professionals that are indeed taking action. In 2012, a growing number of entities, such as the US National Institute of Standards and Technologies (NIST), are designing guidelines for protecting systems, which include recommendations for securing these very basic but highly privileged platform components.

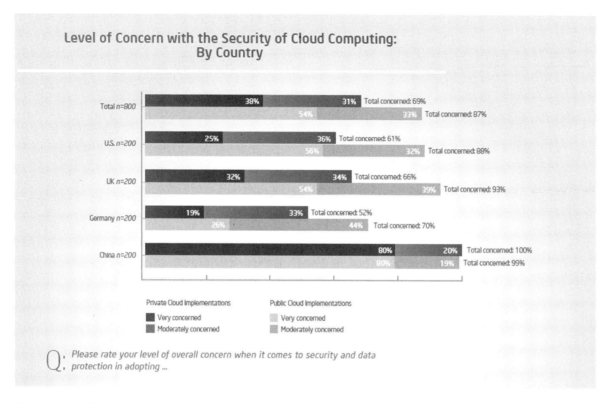

Figure 8-1. *Addressing the need for security in private and public clouds*[1]

More Protections and Assurance

Even as these recommendations from security specialists take form, there is a growing recognition even among the nonsecurity specialists that BIOS is not the only worry. There is the interesting phenomenon that customers and IT managers who implicitly trust the security of their hypervisor in a basic virtualized system grow much more concerned about the security of that same hypervisor when it is deployed in a cloud environment—particularly in a public cloud infrastructure managed by a third party.

This change in perspective is clearly indicative of a customer base that needs new capabilities and controls—more assurance of the integrity of their environment as they virtualize away traditional control and security structures. They need compensating control capabilities to provide assurances for their own concerns, or to assuage the concerns over risk and provide the proofs of protection and control required by others: their information security management professionals or their auditors.

Given the crucial role played by the hypervisor—after all, this essential software is responsible for managing the underlying hardware, allocating resources such as processor, disk, memory, and I/O to the guest virtual machines and arbitrating accesses and privileges among guests—one would want to have the highest levels of assurance that it is

---

[1]McCann, *"What's Holding the Cloud Back?"* Cloud Security Global IT Survey, sponsored by Intel, May 2012.

indeed uncompromised. This is the rationale for the kind of survey results that appear in Figure 8-2. With this growing awareness and concern has come a corresponding growth in vendors looking to define solutions.

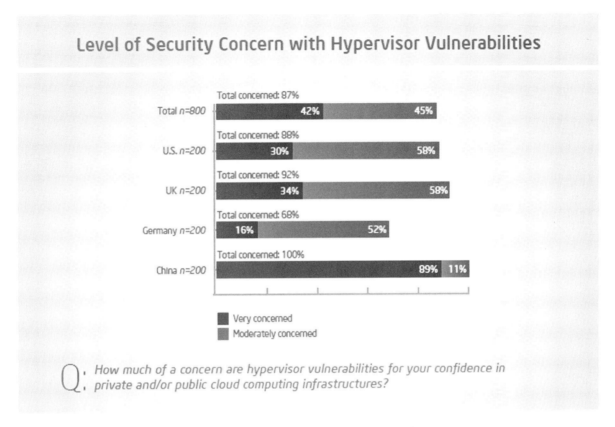

Figure 8-2. *Survey results show concerns over hypervisor integrity across regions[2]*

Along this same line of reasoning, a number of the leading hypervisor platforms have embraced Intel Trusted Execution Technology as a way to allow the hardware and software platforms to work together to provide assurances of integrity. Using cryptographic measurement techniques, applying local whitelist-based policy mechanisms, and creating a tamper-resistant environment, Intel TXT can work with the key platform components to enable a verification mechanism that can help detect alterations in critical BIOS and hypervisor components.

By enforcing this verification on the platform and storing the results in a hardware-based device—the Trusted Platform Module—Intel TXT provides a method for enforcing control for the platform. It also provides visibility into the platform that delivers the assurance benefits needed to meet growing audit and reporting requirements. These requirements are inherent in many corporate IT security policies, as well as rapidly proliferating government and industry security regulations.

Now that Intel TXT is an available, deployable capability on millions of Intel® Xeon® E3, E5, and E7 processor family-based servers from virtually all of the leading OEM[3] and channel providers, a growing ecosystem of software support is emerging to make these visibility and control use models possible. The ecosystem is forming to enable solutions and services to provide these protections and controls. Most of the leading BIOS and hypervisors today

[2]McCann, "*What's Holding the Cloud Back?*" Cloud Security Global IT Survey, sponsored by Intel, May 2012.
[3]For a full list of systems that support Intel TXT, please see www.intel.com/content/www/us/en/architecture-and-technology/trusted-execution-technology/trusted-execution-technology-server-platforms-matrix.html.

are developed in a manner that will allow them to be measured as an integrity check. Virtualization and cloud management platforms can query the host platforms to verify trust status and differentiate trusted, high-integrity platforms from untrusted platforms—the foundations for trusted pools. Security policy engines are being made "trust aware," such that they can work with virtualization and cloud management platforms to control access and workloads based on the platform's trust status. Other key security management tools—such as governance, risk, and compliance (GRC), and security information and event management (SIEM) systems—can report on platform trust and integrity status and events as part of their monitoring and compliance activities. These software stacks enable platform trust to deliver bigger business value beyond basic anti-malware technology.

With these critical links of trust-based use models, platform-level trust can become a full-fledged aspect of an organizations' IT security management portfolio for traditional and virtualized/cloud models. Taken a step further, and given the changing IT architectural models and threat vectors, one could argue that trust is increasingly likely to be a foundational component to these new security models. Intel TXT provides one of the broadest and more widely adoptable mechanisms to enforce trust on platforms and into the enterprise. Learning how to deploy and use this for your organization today will help provide an advantage to reduce near-term risks and meet tactical compliance challenges. It will also provide a solid basis for leveraging related new trust technologies that expand the benefits and provide more protection, control, and visibility for IT security.

Is There Enough to Trust?

There are no silver bullets for security. The threats are too broad, the adversaries too varied, sophisticated and well-resourced to allow a "one size fits all" or single point solution that can stop all threats. Security is a story of multiple lines of defense (or "defense in depth") and of evolution. As threats evolve, so too must the defenses. Trust is no different: it was created to mitigate threats and meet the needs that have been outlined in this book, and it will need to evolve to provide more protection and value over time. The following section discusses how that evolution may play out. Some of this section is speculative and based on early lessons learned from the process of bringing Intel TXT to market with key customers and hardware and software ecosystem partners. While the final destinations and timing might be unclear, and priority or emphasis may influence one evolutionary path over another, the areas of interest seem to be rather universal and worthy of discussion here.

The trust that is available today is innovative, but has limitations that merit discussion. For instance, Intel TXT

- Only measures at launch time.

- Only measures key system BIOS, firmware, and hypervisor (or operating system in a nonvirtualized use) components.

- Works on a whitelist model.

Some would like to argue the benefits of such a limited approach to trust. But the reality is that these limitations—while real—do little to mitigate the value of Intel TXT, as the use models outlined previously should convince the reader. Moreover, these limitations may be overcome by new use and deployment models, complementary security capabilities, and advances as the technology matures. Let's first address the limitations themselves and discuss how material these limitations are and how these limitations can be reduced.

Measures at Launch Time.

First, there is the "launch-time only" aspect of Intel TXT. While Intel TXT actually does provide some protections that keep secrets in memory safe after a trusted launch, the active measurement component of Intel TXT is only invoked at very limited times—at platform launch or restart or when resuming from a sleep mode. Historically and ideally, these would be very infrequent events: customers would often prefer to set up a server, install their software and workloads, and then never have to power it up or down ever again. Alas, this ideal is seldom the reality because customers have software or BIOS updates or facilities changes that required system restarts. But perhaps more interestingly, customers are looking at new, dynamic, virtualized datacenter models that may lead to *increased* frequency of systems being restarted or powered down. With these highly virtualized datacenter models, customers expect to manage systems to maximize power savings, powering systems down in off-peak times—and in such models, customers will get an incremental security benefit in addition to power savings as systems can be verified for integrity upon these restart and resume events.

One last consideration that mitigates this perceived limitation is the role of launch-time integrity enforcement in the overall security portfolio. As noted, no single technology solves all security problems, and as such Intel TXT's primary role is that it provides a solid checkpoint that *complements* the (ideally) many runtime protections such as antivirus and intrusion detection systems. If malware such as a rootkit evades these runtime protections, Intel TXT provides a mechanism that can allow for detection at the next restart/resume event. Otherwise, if they can escape detection by runtime protections, these malicious agents can install themselves into locations that can avoid subsequent detection by these traditional tools—which obviously creates troublesome, long-term vulnerability challenges.

What Intel TXT Measures

The second limitation to assess is what Intel TXT measures. Some would say that measuring BIOS and key firmware, hypervisor, or operating system components does not assure complete platform security. Clearly, no one protection does, and as discussed previously, the proper consideration for Intel TXT is as a complement to runtime security tools. Another aspect of the complementary nature is that Intel TXT will be evaluating aspects and components of a system that are generally weakly protected, if at all, with traditional security tools.

It would be easier to assign far more credence to this concern if the threat environment were not showing very real challenges to these components. Adversaries will find a way to exploit these components into more significant attacks if they are left unprotected. Having hardware-assisted integrity assurances provides an additional strong complementary protection for the IT environment. In the highly consolidated and virtualized IT environment, where a single server no longer hosts a single workload and a compromised host can jeopardize multiple workloads, such protections become even more important.

The Whitelist Approach

The final limitation to address is a potential concern over a whitelist approach vs. the well-established blacklisting approach of so many traditional security tools. Again, one can turn here to the consideration of Intel TXT as a complement to existing tools—and in this case, the alternative approach provides a useful contrast, whereby the different approach eliminates the prospects of an "all security eggs in one basket" approach.

Whitelisting is often challenged by the perception of inflexibility, with good reason. The basic principle of a whitelist security model is that it specifies "known good" elements that one wants to allow. Alternately, a blacklist model is based on stopping all "known bad" elements from executing. Each has its challenges in scale and manageability. But one could argue that in some situations one model is advantageous. The case here is that in the tightly defined boundaries of BIOS, firmware, and hypervisor/operating systems, it is relatively easier for an IT manager to exert tight controls and identify a very finite set of these components that they wish to allow rather than having to identify the essentially infinite set of threats they would like to stop.

Whether one considers these aspects of what Intel TXT provides as limited, it is clear that these capabilities provide additional value to the modern IT security toolbox.

The Evolution of Trust

The previous paragraphs put the capabilities into a suitable context, even as prior chapters outlined how to implement the capabilities into an IT infrastructure, and what controls to expect. In doing so, one hopes that the reader has gained a stronger foundation—a foundation of platform trust—to underpin their datacenter and cloud security model. While this itself is helpful and adds value, there is value in starting today and raising the security bar and being better positioned for further advances in technology. In the future, the basic trust capabilities of the platform can evolve to provide more benefits and greater control through unified hardware, software, and services.

Let's consider where the foundational, launch-time-oriented trust capabilities such as Intel TXT may evolve in the future—either through Intel technology innovation or through evolutionary technology from elsewhere in the software, hardware, and services ecosystem, as shown in Figure 8-3. Three of the more interesting and in-demand areas for innovation are related to delivering the following:

- Trusted guests

- End-to-end trust

- Runtime trust

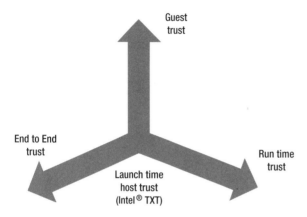

Source: Intel Corporation

Figure 8-3. *The evolution of trust technologies*

Trusted Guest

The first concept is relatively easy to derive from the concept of a trusted host. The premise here is simple: extend the chain of trust established by the hardware at launch, extended through the measured and verified BIOS and hypervisor, and use that trusted base to measure and verify guests as "known good" images. While this cannot be done using Intel TXT hardware solutions today, and there is no significant hardware assistance for such use models today, it is an area of investigation by Intel and the industry in general. But it is not all bad news, for while not rooted in a solid chain of trust, there are currently some promising software-only models that can help verify guest images using whitelist-oriented data management techniques that could be considered quite complementary—especially when run on top of trusted host systems.

End-to-End Trust

The second concept is also easy to grasp if one understands the premise of trusted compute pools already discussed at length in this book. Just as one understands the value in using platform trust attributes to control and manage workloads inside a datacenter or in a cloud environment, one should be able to extend that vision and see a future of trusted clients communicating with trusted clouds. In this manner, platform trust and integrity attributes can benefit both sides of the cloud to client continuum, allowing IT and security managers to establish data and workload access controls based on higher assurances that the client and host have not been compromised. This makes for a very compelling complement to traditional user/role-oriented access control tools. With such a model, security can be based on the users' rights to access data or services, the access device's ability to protect the data or services, and the ability to stop user access to a service or data in the cloud that may have been compromised.

The technologies for such use models are near at hand, and as of mid-2012 proof-of-concept demonstrations of this type of policy enforcement are emerging in the software and service provider ecosystem—including some based on Intel TXT server technologies and McAfee DeepDefender client integrity software on client platforms. Expect a rapid expansion and increased availability and granularity for the types of cloud-to-client trust capabilities that can help enforce data management policies in the coming years.

Runtime Trust

Lastly, trust will also evolve to create better support for runtime-based trust assurances. This chapter has already dedicated space to discussing the need to extend trust and integrity into the runtime space, but has also acknowledged that there is a strong set of products in anti-malware. Intel will continue to evaluate and explore opportunities to use platform hardware enhancements to make trust and integrity assurance more complete, more efficient, and more resistant to attack. As such, one would expect that this evolution will continue over time, with software leading hardware through the development of new use models addressing specific needs and mandates. With the current and expected strong focus for "continuous monitoring" and "continuous compliance" capabilities from entities such as the US government program FedRAMP, the Open Data Center Alliance, and the Cloud Security Alliance, this is a strong area of focus and innovation throughout the industry and across the globe.

The Trust and Integrity "Stack"

Intel has long believed in the need to enhance IT security, and has invested in features such as Intel TXT, Execute Disable (XD) bit, and cryptographic instructions to improve platform and data security. And we've worked with the key security software ecosystem to help assure that these features are enabled and usable to deliver security value to end-user customers. While the collaboration with this broad ecosystem is essential and will continue, in 2010, Intel took a major step and acquired a market leader, McAfee, to move this quest forward. Establishing McAfee as an independent subsidiary allows faster and increasingly deep collaborations between hardware and software capabilities to deliver customers hardened and more efficient, effective security solutions.

Intel and McAfee have established a shared vision for cloud security. Trust and integrity are a critical component of this vision. In this vision, the ability to have a verifiable and auditable high-integrity compute environment can become a reality, with reduced risk from threats, data loss, and downtime, and greater ability to meet compliance requirements.

Increasing the number of enforcement points at multiple layers of the stack will bring higher integrity assurance, especially with additional hardware-enhanced security and software solutions to these areas over time—as discussed in the preceding section. Consider the model from the vision shown in Figure 8-4.

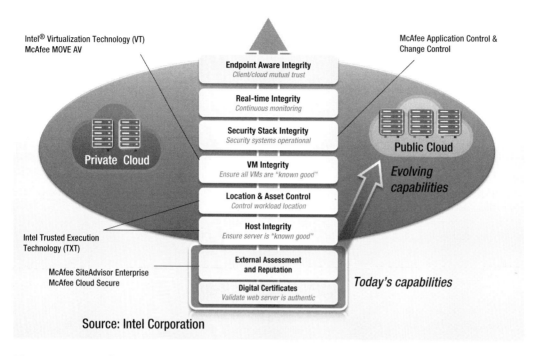

Figure 8-4. *Expanding integrity-based security enforcement points across cloud infrastructures provides more control for IT*

The challenge today is simple: you simply do not know much about any device you may want to connect to—on the Internet or in a cloud. Let's consider an example.

The bottom two items from our diagram are somewhat common today—digital certificates (you see examples when you connect to an online commerce site, for example) or external reputations—if you have a tool like McAfee SiteAdvisor or the like—something that can tell you if a site has been examined for malicious activity. McAfee SiteAdvisor and similar products from other third parties allow you to surf and search the web more safely, avoiding online threats such as spyware, adware, and phishing scams. With the McAfee Cloud Secure program, McAfee enables rigorous security testing, business practice review, compliance certification, and ongoing vulnerability evaluation. Cloud providers and software-as-a-service vendors can demonstrate credible, third-party validated site integrity. *Today, this is essentially all the information you can have when making a connectivity decision.* Unfortunately, that is close to flying blind.

If you want to extend your business to the cloud and make more informed data access and control decisions, you need much more data and control points. Intel and McAfee see a progression of new information that can be provided to allow *much* richer assessments of the security posture of the resources in the cloud. Some of these are being broadly adopted now.

The next step is the host integrity discussion that has been the focus of this book. Using Intel TXT, users are able to verify that the servers they are using have demonstrated integrity. Considering the asset and location control aspect, Intel TXT will also provide a mechanism that will allow a host to store a label in hardware that IT managers or administrators can use to designate the location or other relevant characteristics (customer class, service tier, and so on) of the host server. These attributes can be reported in the same manner as the platform integrity attributes in order to enforce connection or resource allocation policies. One can see how customers can develop use models that are extensions of trusted pools, whereby workloads can be constrained by trust as well as location or asset tag attributes. There are already a number of business and regulatory environments where such extended "boundary controls" based on such physical or logical attributes would be powerful.

Beyond that and further up the stack, McAfee server technologies such as application control and change control work together to reduce overhead on servers and virtual machines while proactively mitigating the risk of data breaches, targeted attacks, and unplanned downtime. These solutions provide proactive security monitoring at the operating system, application, and file level. Additionally, technologies such as the McAfee MOVE Antivirus architecture enhance runtime anti-malware and integrity with an approach that removes the bottlenecks and inefficiencies inherent in the use of scan-based models in virtualized environments. And the previous section discussed how innovative integrators and solution providers can take the Intel and McAfee building blocks to provide end-to-end integrity-based security solutions with a mechanism for mutual verification of trust and integrity between client and cloud to allow for bidirectional control of access to cloud resources.

Although we have discussed the Intel and McAfee joint vision and product synergies in the context of business solutions, rest assured that this is not an Intel/McAfee power play. The preceding text is merely intended to illustrate by concrete example how these two companies see the needs of the market and how we can act together to help address these needs. But the solutions are broader than this—and need to be. Both companies already have leadership positions in datacenter and security markets. Both companies also already have robust ecosystem of third-party partners that provide scalable and interoperable solutions. Both companies are also committed to continue to work with other market and technology leaders and innovators to enhance the robustness, scalability, and completeness of security solutions.

These capabilities promise to deliver greater value to IT and security management professionals as they work to adopt cloud architectures and services. According to data from a McCann Cloud IT security survey sponsored by Intel (Intel 2012), in May 2012:

- Seventy-six percent of IT pros are *very interested* in the ability to measure service providers' security posture in real time

- *Setting and enforcing security policies across clouds* would enhance the confidence of 50 percent of IT pros in adopting public clouds

Starting with a baseline of capabilities enabled in Intel TXT and the use models outlined in this book, and driven by the needs of the market for more and more robust tools for dealing with emerging threats and compliance mandates, Intel and its ecosystem of software and service providers will deliver on-going advancements to hardware and software security for greater control and auditability of cloud and datacenter environments. With these advancements, trust will become a full-fledged complement to today's traditional perimeter and integrity/reputation services for providing security—adding depth and granularity to the controls available to IT and security managers.

Index